NEW DIRECTIONS FOR TEACHING AND LEARNING

Marilla D. Svinicki, *University of Texas, Austin*
EDITOR-IN-CHIEF

D1081929

Using Consultants to Improve Teaching

Christopher Knapper
Queen's University, Kingston, Canada

Sergio Piccinin
University of Ottawa

EDITORS

Number 79, Fall 1999

JOSSEY-BASS PUBLISHERS
San Francisco

Using Consultants to Improve Teaching
Christopher Knapper, Sergio Piccinin (eds.)
New Directions for Teaching and Learning, no. 79
Marilla D. Svinicki, Editor-in-Chief

Microfilm copies of issues and articles are available in 16mm and 35mm, as well as microfiche in 105mm, through University Microfilms Inc., 300 North Zeeb Road, Ann Arbor, Michigan 48106-1346.

ISSN 0271-0633   ISBN 0-7879-4876-4

New Directions for Teaching and Learning is part of The Jossey-Bass Higher and Adult Education Series and is published quarterly by Jossey-Bass Inc., Publishers, 350 Sansome Street, San Francisco, California 94104-1342. Periodicals postage paid at San Francisco, California, and at additional mailing offices. Postmaster: Send address changes to New Directions for Teaching and Learning, Jossey-Bass Inc., Publishers, 350 Sansome Street, San Francisco, California 94104-1342.

New Directions for Teaching and Learning is indexed in College Student Personnel Abstracts, Contents Pages in Education, and Current Index to Journals in Education (ERIC).

Subscriptions cost $58.00 for individuals and $104.00 for institutions, agencies, and libraries. Prices subject to change.

Editorial correspondence should be sent to the editor-in-chief, Marilla D. Svinicki, The Center for Teaching Effectiveness, University of Texas at Austin, Main Building 2200, Austin, TX 78712-1111.

Cover photograph by Richard Blair/Color & Light © 1990.

www.josseybass.com

Printed in the United States of America on acid-free recycled paper containing 100 percent recovered waste paper, of which at least 20 percent is postconsumer waste.

CONTENTS

About This Publication. Since 1980, *New Directions for Teaching and Learning (NDTL)* has brought a unique blend of theory, research, and practice to leaders in postsecondary education. *NDTL* sourcebooks strive not only for solid substance but also for timeliness, compactness, and accessibility.

The series has four goals: to inform readers about current and future directions in teaching and learning in postsecondary education, to illuminate the context that shapes these new directions, to illustrate these new directions through examples from real settings, and to propose ways in which these new directions can be incorporated into still other settings.

This publication reflects the view that teaching deserves respect as a high form of scholarship. We believe that significant scholarship is conducted not only by researchers who report results of empirical investigations but also by practitioners who share disciplined reflections about teaching. Contributors to *NDTL* approach questions of teaching and learning as seriously as they approach substantive questions in their own disciplines, and they deal not only with pedagogical issues but also with the intellectual and social context in which these issues arise. Authors deal on the one hand with theory and research and on the other with practice, and they translate from research and theory to practice and back again.

About This Volume. In the current issue the topic of peer consultation is addressed from a theoretical, an empirical, and a practical perspective. With increasing calls for accountability of faculty, the use of peers as teaching consultants can help us monitor our own effectiveness as professionals.

MARILLA D. SVINICKI, editor-in-chief, is director of the Center for Teaching Effectiveness at the University of Texas, Austin.

EDITORS' NOTES

If you are a professor who needs help with a teaching problem, the best place to start is to talk with a knowledgeable colleague. That simple idea is the basis for instructional consultation. Conversations about teaching take place hundreds of times each day at colleges and universities all over the world. But with the advent of teaching and learning centers some thirty years ago, the consultation process became more systematic and formalized.

Provision of one-on-one advice on teaching is a key service offered by many faculty development centers, especially in North America. Such advice is not just remedial and problem focused but is also targeted to those good teachers who wish to try new methods that will enhance teaching and learning effectiveness. Some centers have developed careful protocols for the consultation they offer, often including a process of needs assessment, strategic planning for change, and evaluation through classroom visits and feedback from students. Another important development has been the growth of peer consultation—trained colleagues advising fellow teachers—sometimes functioning independently of the teaching center, but using systems devised by professional instructional developers.

Instructional consultation is an activity we almost take for granted, yet it is widespread enough to deserve discussion and critical scrutiny. That was the purpose of a session we coordinated at a fascinating conference sponsored by the International Consortium for Educational Development (held in Austin, Texas, April 1998). ICED is a consortium of fifteen national organizations for educational developers, including the Professional and Organizational Development Network (POD) in the United States and the Canadian Society for Teaching and Learning in Higher Education (STLHE). The conference provided an intriguing international and multicultural perspective on faculty development issues, and our own session, titled "Models of Instructional Consultation," included presenters from the United States, Canada, Australia, and Britain. The ensuing discussion was lively, and several members of the audience offered their own ideas on instructional consultation. They were invited to join the original presenters in writing up their ideas for the present book.

This issue of *NDTL* begins with our introduction to the origins of and rationale for instructional consulting. We also raise some important questions about the conceptual underpinnings for consulting practice. Next, Owen Hicks gives a very useful framework for classifying consultation approaches in terms of their focus, clientele, outcomes, and recognition for those taking part. For readers anxious to get started, Barbara Millis explains three highly practical approaches to peer consultation: classroom observation, student focus groups, and small group instructional diagnosis.

The following three chapters all describe consultation systems with somewhat different approaches and in different institutional settings. Michael Kerwin deals with consultation across a statewide system of colleges in Kentucky; Milton Cox writes about peer consultation through the very successful learning communities that have been in place for thirty years at Miami University, Ohio; and Liz Beaty describes a British approach to consultation through action learning. Gunnar Handal's chapter offers a uniquely European perspective on collegiality in higher education and raises some provocative questions about our obligations to serve as *critical friends* to our peers on matters of teaching and research.

The crucial question of consultation outcomes is addressed by Sergio Piccinin, who discusses evidence for impacts on teaching effectiveness and describes the results of a comprehensive study of his own. Cynthia Weston and Lynn McAlpine raise interesting issues about the locale and responsibility for instructional consultation and whether we should move away from generic programs to discipline-based services. The volume ends with an overview of further resources on consultation, including publications, organizations, and electronic media.

Although all the authors are agreed on the value of consulting with others to improve teaching and learning, they vary considerably in the way they believe this can best be done. We hope that this volume will stimulate discussion and reflection about a largely unexamined activity, but one that plays a crucial role in making teaching a truly collegial part of our academic work.

Christopher Knapper
Sergio Piccinin
Editors

CHRISTOPHER KNAPPER *is professor of psychology and director of the Instructional Development Centre at Queen's University, Kingston, Canada.*

SERGIO PICCININ *is professor of psychology and director of the Centre for University Teaching at the University of Ottawa, Canada.*

1   *Instructional consulting can improve teaching, but should be underpinned by conceptually based training in appropriate skills.*

Consulting About Teaching: An Overview

Christopher Knapper, Sergio Piccinin

University teaching is almost unique among professions because its practitioners generally receive no advanced training for their major role and, once appointed, usually teach in isolation from the scrutiny of colleagues. Here we have a sort of double jeopardy in the sense that teaching is largely an amateur activity (in both the good and bad sense of that word) and is also an essentially private one, at least where colleagues are concerned.

In most professions there are quite stringent training and accreditation standards. Indeed, universities are a major source of that training. Professions also have traditions of reflection and discussion about appropriate professional practice (Schön, 1983). In part this is achieved through conversations with colleagues about job-related issues; in this way, professionals learn about new developments and improved procedures. But there is also a well-established tradition in many fields of seeking advice from specialists—consultants—from both inside and outside the work organization. These individuals are widely used in business and industry to provide advice when problems arise or when the organization is facing new circumstances. Indeed universities themselves frequently employ consultants to advise on administrative systems, and many research grants make provision for payment to consultants on technical matters.

Until about thirty years ago the idea of providing specialist advice on university teaching was largely unknown. But with the spread of faculty and instructional development centers, starting in the 1970s, there was a recognition that university teaching is a vitally important activity that needs to be learned—and learned not simply by trial and error but through organized activities and professional expertise.

Although the United States undoubtedly boasts the largest number of faculty development centers, university teaching and learning units exist in countries throughout the Western world. Many of them offer some type of individual consultation for the improvement of teaching though, as Hicks, Beaty, and Handal point out in the present volume, such a service is much more common among universities in North America than in Europe or Australia. Typically, an individual faculty member approaches the center for help with an instructional problem. With very simple issues the matter might be dealt with in a brief phone call or by written advice in the form of a book or brochure. But usually there is a meeting or series of meetings between the teacher and the adviser, often supplemented by a classroom visit in which the adviser watches the teacher at work and sometimes by consultations with a sample of students enrolled in the course concerned.

What are the issues and problems that cause faculty to seek advice about their teaching? What skills do developers need to make the process useful, and how are such skills acquired? Is there any conceptual basis for the consultation process itself and the advice on teaching and learning that is offered? Should consultation be organized centrally and use a generic approach, or is it better to work through and for individual disciplines and departments? Who should serve as consultants: expert developers or peers? How effective is such consultation, and what impact does it have upon the quality of teaching and learning in the institution? These are some of the questions that this volume addresses.

The Conceptual Basis for Consultation

What sorts of problems do teachers bring to consultants, and what strategies do consultants use to help tackle them? In fact there is surprisingly little empirical evidence on the identity of the issues discussed in the consulting process. Anecdotal data suggest that teachers seek help in the face of poor student evaluations or when an immediate problem arises in the classroom, for example an inability to engage students in discussion or to end disruptive behavior. It would be helpful to have more complete information on issues and problems that give rise to requests for help. Even better would be evidence on what strategies are most effective for different types of problem. Piccinin's work, reported in this volume, offers a beginning, but more research is needed in a variety of institutions.

We know rather more about the strategies used by consultants, because they are often described in some detail in faculty development manuals (such as the ones listed in the final chapter). A common approach is for the consultant to clarify teaching goals, encourage reflection about aims and methods, observe teaching, offer personal feedback, and sometimes arrange for feedback from students. On the whole, consultants receive little systematic training for their role—an irony, because the lack of training in teaching for faculty is the very reason such consultation is needed in the first place! A second irony is that where training is offered it is usually for peer consultants, not professional faculty developers. The chapters by Beaty, Cox, Kerwin, and Millis give full and helpful information about strategies that might be used by peer consultants to assess and enhance teaching.

What is the underlying rationale for consulting? In one sense it seems a matter of common sense, based on the reasonable psychological principle that performance of any task can benefit from knowledgeable feedback, especially when coupled with workable strategies for change and ongoing monitoring of the effect of such change. This is the basis of much coaching in sports and the arts, and the way we learn many new skills in everyday life—such as learning a novel computer application, improving our golf swing, or mastering a Mozart piano sonata. It seems plausible that such strategies might be effective in the case of teaching, and indeed Piccinin demonstrates that they are. Certainly the consultation processes described in this volume are an improvement on feedback from student evaluations and from peers on tenure and promotion committees, which often comes too late to be of use and unaccompanied by any practical suggestions for change and improvement.

However, given the long history, huge scale, and considerable importance (social, psychological, economic) of university teaching, it seems strange that we should rely on common sense to guide the consulting process, even if it is more effective than doing nothing. Is there not a conceptual basis for instructional consulting, parallel to the rationale for the reflective practitioner articulated by Schön in the case of business professionals? In particular, are there principles of good teaching and learning that might guide the consultant's work?

Some developers would probably resist such an idea, because it violates their belief in a value-free approach to consultation, perhaps equivalent to client-centered therapy, in which the teacher's goals are preeminent, instructional problems are defined by the person seeking advice, and strategies are selected accordingly, even if the consultant has private doubts about them. Hence advice might be offered about more dynamic lecturing, even if the consultant believes lecturing is generally ineffective or inappropriate for this teaching situation. Interestingly, good student evaluation instruments are not value-free, in the sense that the questions they include are based on empirical studies of aspects of teaching that students deem important. And there is no shortage of prescriptions for the components of effective teaching in higher education. One example is the list of "seven principles for good practice in undergraduate education" developed by Chickering and Gamson (1987). Another is the characteristics of instruction developed by Ramsden, which are thought to foster deep learning (Ramsden and Entwistle, 1981). A useful step for the future would be for those involved in instructional consulting to spell out the conceptual basis for their work, dealing both with the consulting strategies they use to identify problems and effect change and with the conceptions of teaching that underpin the advice they offer. Many businesses and services now offer a *charter of rights* for consumers; perhaps the time is ripe for a similar warranty from consultants and educational developers!

Who Offers and Seeks Consultation?

We know rather more about instructional consultants and their clients. Consulting is done both by educational developers and increasingly by ordinary faculty. This is partly a matter of logistics (there are simply too many seeking individual consultation for developers to cope) and partly of philosophy, as Handal has described so well in his chapter on the *critical friend*. Weston and McAlpine also make an interesting argument that teaching consultation needs to be increasingly discipline based if it is to effect change in teaching methods and curriculum.

We should not overlook the role played by students in the consulting process, both through the teaching evaluations students complete and through the use of students in focus groups to critique a course and offer suggestions for change. Indeed, in one of the earliest instructional consultation programs, the Clinic to Improve University Teaching at the University of Massachusetts, the consultation was provided primarily by trained graduate students.

Those seeking advice come from all faculties and ranks, as Piccinin's research has shown, with an understandable tendency for more junior faculty to become involved; Boice's work (1992) has shown the importance of faculty's seeking help with teaching early in their careers. Although most consulting is one-on-one, there are also some promising approaches using groups of faculty. Consulting need not even be face-to-face; it can sometimes be done by telephone or through the mechanism of an electronic discussion forum, where problems can be posed (sometimes anonymously), answered, and debated.

Consultation and Accountability

Most of those who seek consulting come of their own free will, and indeed most faculty development centers are reluctant to accept referrals, even from a well-meaning department, unless it is clear that the teacher is motivated to improve and is not being coerced. Consultation is largely a confidential process, although it is partly in the public domain because it involves students. It certainly seems unlikely that consultation would do any good if faculty were conscripted to take part. Yet Handal has raised the interesting issue of whether we might be better off with instructional consultation that is collegial, open, and seen as part of our obligation to the institution and the academic profession at large (and, it might be added, to students and society). He makes an intriguing parallel with research, where peer review is accepted and valued as a mutual responsibility.

The past decade has seen increasing complaints from the public and politicians about the quality of teaching in higher education and the lack of training for practitioners. Many countries have introduced systems to assess the quality of academic programs, and there has even been discussion of accreditation of university teachers. Britain has had a voluntary scheme for certification of university teachers for some time, developed by the Staff and Educational Development Association. With the establishment there of the Institute for Teaching and Learning, accreditation will probably become mandatory.

Whether or not training and ongoing educational development becomes a requirement elsewhere, it seems likely that there will be increasing pressure to "professionalize" university teaching. If so, then one component of training and development could well involve seeking help from an expert consultant, planning for change, and documenting the effects of that change. Because real change is likely to require attention to teaching content (curriculum) as well as to instructional methods, it seems probable that involvement in consultation will become a professional obligation, comparable to serving on a committee or acting as referee for a research grant. If so, then this might help overcome two dilemmas faced by faculty developers—that seeking help is in some way demeaning and an admission of incompetence and that those most in need of help may be reluctant to seek it.

With all the caveats about the need for appropriate training, better research, and the need for a conceptual basis, can we conclude that consulting is a worthwhile activity? For faculty developers the answer must be yes, because it is a service that faculty demand, that generates goodwill for those we are able to help, and that has been shown to be effective. Despite the fact that one-on-one consultation is time consuming and demanding, the payoff can be considerable in view of the number of students a single instructor teaches. For colleagues there are also considerable benefits, not only from the satisfaction derived from receiving and giving help but also from making teaching a more professional and public activity.

References

Boice, R. *The New Faculty Member: Supporting and Fostering Professional Development.* San Francisco: Jossey-Bass, 1992.

Chickering, A. W., and Gamson, Z. F. "Seven Principles in Undergraduate Education." Special insert to *The Wingspread Journal*, 1987, *9* (2).

Ramsden, R., and Entwistle, N. J. "Effects of Academic Departments on Students' Approaches to Learning." *British Journal of Educational Psychology*, 1981, *51*, 368–383.

Schön, D. A. *The Reflective Practitioner: How Professionals Think in Action.* New York: Basic Books, 1983.

CHRISTOPHER KNAPPER is professor of psychology and director of the Instructional Development Centre at Queen's University, Kingston, Canada.

SERGIO PICCININ is professor of psychology and director of the Centre for University Teaching at the University of Ottawa.

2

A conceptual framework for consultation on teaching embraces four crucial components of the process: access, focus, recognition, and outcomes.

A Conceptual Framework for Instructional Consultation

Owen Hicks

This chapter provides a conceptual framework for consultation on teaching, first exploring the meaning of the term, then examining four key aspects of the process: access, focus, recognition, and outcomes. Different forms of consultation are considered in relation to this framework, along with their application to various target groups within the university. Among the questions addressed are how we ensure that those who seek consultation know of its availability and are able to access it, who should set the consultation agenda, how we recognize and ensure adequate resources for effective consultation, and how we know that a model of consultation is effective.

Defining Consultation for Instructional Development

An analysis of the international literature on instructional consultation shows noticeable differences in terminology and definition, influenced largely by the dominant paradigm operating in each country or region. In the United States terms such as *instructional consultation* and *teaching consultant* are commonly used. Lenze (1996) describes instructional consultation as involving the provision of an outside, unbiased perspective (that of the faculty developer) on a faculty member's teaching. According to Lenze, consultation usually offers face-to-face interaction and individualized attention. Brinko (1997) sees instructional consultation as a formative process involving a consultant visiting a classroom, collecting information about the teaching, and then feeding this back to the instructor.

On the basis of available research, Lenze (1996) regards instructional consultation as a preferable instructional development strategy to other common approaches, such as workshops, grants for instructional improvement, advice from colleagues, and provision of resource materials. And in a brochure titled "The Individual Consultation Process," the Center for Teaching Effectiveness at the University of Texas at Austin noted that, despite the fact that it is time consuming, consultation is one of the most effective services a center can provide to enhance teaching. Menges stated his belief that "no service provided by teaching centers has greater potential for producing deep and enduring effects on teachers and teaching" (Brinko and Menges, 1997, p. v).

Canadian references often use the term *peer consultation* (which might in some instances be equated with Lenze's phrase, "colleagues helping colleagues"). Again the focus is personal and individual but usually provided by a teaching colleague rather than an expert faculty developer. Peer consultation illustrates what Brinko (1997, p. vii) identifies as one of the two most common approaches to instructional consultation, the *collaborative model*. In this approach the consultant acts as a facilitator of change. In the *prescription model*, the consultant identifies, diagnoses, and solves problems. One of the earliest structured peer consultation programs was that introduced at the University of Alberta, Edmonton, in 1981 (Roed, 1995).

In Australia and the United Kingdom, although these sorts of services are certainly provided, the term instructional consultation is not common. In Australia, one-to-one assistance to faculty forms a far less significant component of faculty development than in North America. Much more common are the other forms of instructional development in Lenze's (1996) list.

Given these different definitions and emphases, perhaps a helpful way forward would be to accept instructional consultation as the general process and add some qualifications according to who is involved. Thus peer consultation could be seen as an identifiable subset of instructional consultation, one involving colleagues from the same or a different discipline. The Alberta program matches individuals with consultants from a different department or discipline, seeing the client as the expert on subject matter and the consultant as focused on the more general processes of teaching. This differentiation according to who performs the role of consultant is not intended to imply that collegial relationships cannot exist between instructional developers and faculty or that colleagues cannot also be experts. However, it does allow us to consider these types of consultation to be distinct and to explore the differences in the relationships. It also has the advantage of not immediately casting the instructional developer into the prescription model described by Brinko (1997).

A further complication to our understanding of instructional consultation relates to the degree of formality, focus, and intensity that should be attached to the term. It could be argued that by far the greatest amount of instructional consultation takes the form of quite incidental and informal advice sought and received by colleagues in the faculty common room or the corridor. Should this be included in an audit of instructional consultation? It can be argued that a continuum exists from informal peer interaction at one extreme, through structured peer-to-peer consultation, to instructional developer guided consultation at the other extreme.

A typical interaction of the latter kind is described by Menges, Weimer, and Associates (1996, p. 250). It involves a teacher concerned about difficulties in asking and responding to student questions consulting with an expert from the college teaching center. The consultant listens to the problem, interacts with the class to gain further information, provides feedback to the teacher, and gives advice as requested, then revisits the class to observe the change in teaching practice. A generic variation of this model occurs when an academic contacts an academic developer in a central unit to seek advice with a teaching problem, often after receiving adverse feedback from student evaluations.

The University of Alberta provides an example of a peer consultation program that sits somewhere in the middle of the continuum. The program is a confidential service to instructors who work with a trained colleague to change some aspect of their teaching. The purpose is to discover ways to improve teaching and learning, and the results are not intended as an evaluation of the instructor's competence. The peer consultant can provide advice from his or her own experience, and also act as a conduit for information from students, a sounding board for the instructor's concerns and ideas about teaching, and a source of suggestions for change. Each consultation is tailored to the situation but often includes a classroom visit by the consultant, videotaping part of a class, interviews with groups of students, and a written report containing a diagnostic assessment.

It is clearly a matter of definition, but we also need to ask where consultation begins and other forms of instructional development end. For example, can consultation involve a whole group, as when participants in workshops or interest groups meet to discuss common teaching problems and solutions? Perhaps what best defines instructional consultation is its focus and the nature of the interaction involved. The focus is the process of instruction, usually the immediate practicalities of everyday teaching: how to teach, possibly what to teach, but not the actual nature of what is being taught. The nature of the content or discipline will have an impact on the appropriateness of various teaching and learning strategies, and it cannot be ignored. However, content is generally seen as the province of the individual faculty member and not the consultant.

The nature of the interaction is such that it can involve one or more participants, individually or as a group, seeking assistance or advice from another party regarding an aspect of their teaching. This is most commonly a one-on-one interaction. Although instructional developers may have an established process for consultation, critical here is the fact that it is the "seekers" who, initially at least, are proactive in initiating the process and setting the agenda.

It could be argued that such a definition, based on the focus of the consultation and the nature of the interaction, includes almost all faculty development activities other than formal structured programs. However, workshops, grants, and resource materials (the other instructional intervention categories of Lenze [1996]) would certainly be excluded from the above prescription.

Access to Instructional Consultation

How do we ensure that those who are seeking the consultation service know of its availability and are able to access it? Most centers for teaching and learning in universities and colleges advertise their services through brochures or a Web site. Yet this does not ensure that those most in need of help will know of its availability. And it is often those who may need the consultation most who are least likely to seek it out.

Accessing instructional consultation has special challenges. Whereas structured courses require registration at a particular time, a request for consultation can occur whenever the faculty member initiates it. This gives the advantage of flexibility but also requires the individual to decide when would be a good time or when the situation is bad enough to prompt a request for help. Hence flexibility may well lead to inaction, with other demands on the teacher's time squeezing out what may seem optional, something that can wait. To counter such a tendency, special promotion of instructional consultation could occur at critical times through the academic year—though not preventing faculty from seeking assistance at any other time. The second week of the semester, when the realities of teaching problems begin to hurt, may be a good time. And advertising that seeks to counter the inclination to procrastinate ("Don't wait till it's too late") can be another useful strategy.

Access may be constrained by a perceived stigma attached to what might be seen as remedial assistance to faculty unable to teach effectively. Once again, marketing to counter this impression may be necessary. Many teachers with limited skills are unlikely to access instructional consultation if doing so reinforces a perception of their inadequacy. Being able to cite recognized good teachers who have made use of consultation services to improve their teaching could assist significantly in promoting consultation to a wider group of faculty. Here perhaps the slogan should be "with teaching you've never learned it all."

Some of the different forms of consultation present unique access difficulties. Incidental consultation from supportive peers depends on the existence locally of colleagues willing and competent to assist. Consultation between peers is likely to be more accidental and casual, dependent on other processes that bring together those seeking assistance and those able to provide it. And it is likely that those in greatest need will have least access to colleagues. A strong teaching department is likely to provide good support to peers in an organizational culture in which teaching is valued and challenges are shared. The converse is likely to be true in a department that does not value teaching highly. In this environment consultation is likely to be most beneficial, but informed peers willing and available to provide the consultation needed are not likely to be available. It would make an interesting study to analyze the pattern of usage of consulting opportunities. We might hypothesize that peer consultants would be drawn from strong teaching departments and accessed by those from weak teaching departments unable or unwilling to provide the support and expertise locally.

It needs to be recognized that except for the likely unworkable situation of compulsory instructional consultation, it is possible to provide help only for those who willingly participate in the process. This may appear a more significant limitation than it is in reality. Clearly, the nature of any academic development activity is such that the participants must be willing and open to learn. Instructional consultation is no different in this regard.

In many institutions the proportion of academic staff seeking instructional consultation is quite small (mercifully perhaps, because most instructional development centers would find it difficult to meet a greater demand). Is this group an accurate reflection of those able to benefit from the service? If not, are the needs of those not accessing instructional consultation being met in some other way? A search of the literature has shown no published evidence about the level of need for instructional consultation. Should this service be seen as a *residual activity* offered to those identified as struggling with their teaching or those self-starters keen to improve beyond their already adequate level of competence? Alternatively, should consultation be seen as a *universal activity* that all faculty should participate in from time to time? The first approach may allow consultation to be provided to those in greatest need. The latter approach offers the prospect of a greater impact on teaching and more widespread acceptance of the benefits of consultation.

One of the strongest challenges to instructional consultation is likely to come from those who argue that its impact is too limited, involving too few willing faculty privileged enough to avail themselves of the service. Wide use of instructional consultation, it could be argued, is functional only for institutions affluent enough to provide the resources and for faculty who have the motivation and time to take advantage of the service. Conversely, letting teaching problems go unattended can have major negative impacts on many hundreds of students and consequently on the reputation of an entire department or institution.

The Focus of Instructional Consultation

Who sets the agenda for the consultation? Can consultation help address issues and problems not currently recognized by teachers but perceived by others as requiring attention? The literature on instructional consultation almost always assumes that the power to set the agenda will lie with the academic seeking advice and assistance. To be effective this requires significant powers of self-reflection and at least some initial self-diagnosis on the part of the faculty member. Of course some conversations about teaching take place quite informally between faculty. But it is uncommon for a more experienced colleague to observe another's teaching unless specifically asked. And any attempt to impose instructional consultation could be seen as a grave violation of academic freedom.

Although there may be examples, possibly following a formal review process, of faculty being compelled to consult with an instructional developer, they are rare. If consultation is to be at all effective, the consultant and faculty member must first negotiate a communication process and determine the issues the teacher is willing and motivated to address. Structured programs of consultation, though usually established and supported by a center for teaching and learning, still require voluntary participation by faculty members. The developer needs to negotiate the agenda with the individual affected and gain that teacher's acceptance for the process.

One of the limitations of instructional consultation is that it is likely to be responsive and reactive in its focus, correcting perceived problems of individual academics. Because it is often perceived as remedial, offering help when something is going wrong, there may be a tendency to avoid suggesting changes that are genuinely innovative or experimental or that break new ground in teaching and learning. Instead consultants are more likely to rely on the best of what has come before. Hence it is important that centers also offer other instructional development strategies that are more forward looking.

What of the serious inadequacies of departments in which the teaching is moribund yet the faculty have little awareness of this situation? Incidental consultation between colleagues is unlikely to occur here, and even if it did the situation could possibly be likened to the blind leading the blind. Cross-disciplinary instructional consultation might be one solution, but it is likely to be new junior staff with less influence in the department who seek external help. Hence change would be a slow and difficult process in a culture possibly hostile to the need to improve teaching quality. In such situations the university may be better off with a more comprehensive and intrusive strategy.

If consultation is left to the initiative of the individual faculty member, can it be an adequate mechanism for institutional improvement? At the University of Western Australia some years ago, a survey showed that 84 percent of academic staff saw themselves in the top 25 percent of teachers

and that there was a degree of complacency about the need to improve (Eaton and Schmidt-Posner, 1992). It seems unlikely that faculty who have such positive self-images would seek out consultation. More cynically, it could be argued that peer consultation in this environment could actually reinforce and perpetuate poor quality teaching.

What about consultation about new teaching methods, where there is presumably less stigma attached to admitting ignorance and the need to learn new skills? For example, might not consultation on the use of multimedia and information technology be effective, perhaps in the process leading to reflection about broader teaching goals and methods? This suggests the need, possibly at an institutional level, for targeted offerings of consultation on particular themes that are inherently interesting or problematic, such as the use of technology in teaching, strategies for motivating students and of effective and efficient assessment. Such a targeted approach would require a pool of the relevant expertise and a marketing strategy to publicize the service. This is clearly an approach that lies on the right of the continuum mentioned earlier, and equivalent to Brinko's (1997) prescription model.

Recognition of Instructional Consultation

Given that consultation is usually a hidden (or at least less public), less tangible aspect of the work of academic development units, in times of scarce resources teaching and learning centers need to take particular care that efforts in consultation are recognized by those who provide the funding as well as by those who directly benefit from the service. This is often made difficult by academics wishing to keep confidential their requests for help. In some instances individuals seek consultation to avoid the public exposure of participating in a structured course on teaching where they fear the public exposure of their skills might be embarrassing. Consultation gives them a more discreet and personal way of addressing concerns.

Although it is important to respect confidentiality, some form of recognition is essential for the providers of instructional consultation, especially if they are volunteers. Such recognition may be a tangible or intangible acknowledgment. It may take the form of monetary payment, which occurs in a de facto way for instructional developers employed to provide consultation as part of their role. For peer consultants recognition is more likely to be a balance of intrinsic and extrinsic (nonmonetary) rewards. Many testify to the personal benefits they gain, and the improvements in their own teaching that occur as a result of acting as advisers to colleagues. In some universities peer consultants are recognized through certification that they can then cite as a form of community service and use to advantage in seeking promotion.

Recognition for those receiving consultation is more tricky, especially if the service is seen as largely remedial. But faculty members could see instructional consultation in a new light if it were known that they could obtain some sort of extrinsic credit for participating. Although this would need to be optional, certification for participation in what might be called the "Teaching Enhancement Consultation Program" might be effective in some institutions. Such certification could identify the particular skills improved through the consultation process and could be documented on a curriculum vitae or a teaching portfolio.

Outcomes of Instructional Consultation

Of critical importance in instructional consultation is follow-through. Too often the consultation process ends prematurely. Often instructional consultation mechanisms support faculty through the problem identification and diagnostic phases of improving their teaching and then leave them largely on their own to specify the solution, put it into practice, and evaluate the impact of the change. It is essential that support is available right through to the point where the faculty can recognize the change they have instituted in their teaching and the impact this has had on their students' learning. This leads to the whole question of benefits and outcomes.

The specifics of instructional consultation are likely to be kept confidential between the consultant and the faculty member. Hence cause and effect links between instructional development and teaching improvement are difficult to prove. The often piecemeal one-to-one approach of traditional consultation makes it hard to aggregate outcomes at an institutional level. Although throughput measures such as simple head counts give some information, they may bear little relationship to outcomes. Personal testimony appears to remain the strongest argument for continuing to support instructional consultation in most universities. Belief in the effectiveness of instructional consultation, in Australian universities at least, is largely an act of faith, based on hearsay evidence and the fact that the demand for consultation almost always exceeds the availability of formally recognized consulting services. It may be that often what is sought is relatively unsophisticated advice and assistance, almost guaranteed to lead to improvement, but nonetheless valuable for both teachers and their students.

What do we assume to be the results of instructional consultation? Surely the ultimate aim is to bring about better student learning by enabling faculty to improve their teaching. We might hope that students would learn more quickly and easily, have a better understanding of difficult concepts in their courses, and find learning more enjoyable and fulfilling. This might be demonstrated by improved student evaluations of teaching, higher grades on exams, or lower attrition rates. Can instructional consultation deliver? Anecdotal evidence suggests it can, at least for particular individuals. And the empirical evidence from Australia, Canada, and the United States, reviewed by Piccinin in this volume, shows that those seeking consultation do in fact improve their teaching.

Future Directions

The chapter so far has focused largely on individual, one-to-one consultation. But group-focused peer consultation and the fostering of a culture of mutual consultation among colleagues are strategies that may well prove more cost effective. There is less discussion of these approaches in the literature, but the chapters by Beaty and Kerwin in this volume describe such programs at institutions in Britain and the United States. At the University of Western Australia, the Innovative Learning Forum is a grassroots group of academics who meet regularly to discuss aspects of their teaching and to swap solutions to problems they have confronted. This cross-disciplinary group also operates an electronic discussion list. A further example can be found in the Teaching Reflection and Collaboration (TRAC) program at the Queensland University of Technology, which involves a network of special interest groups who meet regularly to discuss teaching and learning issues and plan solutions (Scott and Weeks, 1998). Although TRAC is coordinated by the faculty development unit, the network is essentially a devolved responsibility, with group activities motivated by the needs of group participants.

Computer-mediated consultation provides another direction for the future. Communication between consultant and faculty member can and does occur through a variety of media such as telephone and e-mail. The potential of peer consultation through electronic discussion groups is obvious. Many such groups currently exist and provide good examples of mutual consultation. Many societies established to further teaching and learning in higher education operate e-mail lists for this purpose, for example the Society for Teaching and Learning in Higher Education in Canada, and the Professional and Organizational Development Network in the United States. In Australia such lists exist nationally and locally. There are also other examples of interactive computer-mediated consultation, such as the Teaching and Learning Technology Resource, a Web-based database at the University of Western Australia. This puts academics in touch with the expertise of their peers across campus to assist them in making effective use of technology in their teaching. The LEAP project at the University of Adelaide in South Australia has a similar function. Although the value of the personal interaction of conventional consultation should not be underestimated, technology will undoubtedly play an increasing role in the instructional consultation processes of the future.

References

Brinko, K. T. "The Interactions of Teaching Improvement." In K. T. Brinko and R. J. Menges (eds.), *Practically Speaking: A Sourcebook for Instructional Consultants in Higher Education.* Stillwater, Okla.: New Forums Press, 1997.

Brinko, K. T., and Menges, R. J. (eds.). *Practically Speaking: A Sourcebook for Instructional Consultants in Higher Education.* Stillwater, Okla.: New Forums Press, 1997.

Eaton, E., and Schmidt-Posner, J. "Towards Academic Excellence: A Study of Academic Staff Views About Feedback on Teaching and Values About Teaching and Research." Unpublished report, prepared for the Academic Staff Development Committee, University of Western Australia, Perth, 1992.

Lenze, L. F. "Instructional Development: What Works?" *National Education Association, Office of Higher Education Update,* 1996, 2 (4), 1–4.

Menges, R. J., Weimer, M., and Associates. *Teaching on Solid Ground: Using Scholarship to Improve Practice.* San Francisco: Jossey-Bass, 1996.

Roed, B. *The Peer Consultation Program at the University of Alberta.* Edmonton, Canada: University Teaching Services, University of Alberta, 1995.

Scott, D. C., and Weeks, P. "The TRAC Network: Cross-Disciplinary Teaching and Learning Research and Deliberation." Paper presented at the International Consortium for Educational Development conference, Austin, Tex., Apr. 19–22, 1998.

OWEN HICKS *is director of the Centre for Staff Development at the University of Western Australia and president of the Higher Education Research and Development Society of Australasia.*

3

Small group instructional diagnosis, student focus groups, and classroom observation are three procedures faculty can use for effective peer consultation.

Three Practical Strategies for Peer Consultation

Barbara J. Millis

Assessment of program, course, and instructor performance has become an increasing concern at many academic institutions, fueled by a number of forces. These include (1) general demands, within the academy and outside, for accountability, (2) state or provincial legislative scrutiny, (3) family pressures for *value added* educational returns, and (4) new accreditation standards, such as the Accreditation Board for Engineering and Technology's new emphasis on an evaluation process driven by measurable learning outcomes.

Institutions charged with designing and documenting outcomes assessment are finding that systematic peer review can provide valuable qualitative evidence of teaching effectiveness. A closed door policy, sometimes defended on the grounds of academic freedom, is no longer a viable option on many campuses. Like their faculty development colleagues, faculty members can become conversant with professional ways to assess and improve the overall effectiveness of teachers, courses, and programs.

At the United States Air Force Academy (USAFA), the Center for Educational Excellence (CEE) offers three consultation options. Because of increasing demands and a small staff, we can provide such services only with the assistance of trained faculty consultants. Besides classroom observations (often coupled with videotaping), we use two types of structured student interviews to gather student-generated assessment data: focus groups and small group instructional diagnosis (SGID).

All three approaches involve a four-step process. First, there is an initial interview during which faculty members discuss with the consultant such key issues as the overall course objectives, the nature of the course, their teaching philosophy, the teaching methodologies they most often employ, their perceptions of the students and the course, their specific concerns or expectations, and the reasons behind the visit or interview. Second is the observation or student interview itself. Third comes the feedback session or debriefing, during which the consultants and teachers (often including other department members when multi-section courses or program development are involved) discuss and interpret the data and plan future changes. In the final stage, faculty share the data with students and discuss ways to strengthen the course or program.

Small Group Instructional Diagnosis (SGID)

At the Air Force Academy SGID is used to gather valuable data on single classes to help individual instructors improve their teaching. Departments, usually through course directors responsible for coordinating all sections of core courses, also use them to guide curriculum revisions. Based on initial research by Joseph Clark (Clark & Redmond, 1982), practitioners such as Diamond (1988) and Nyquist and Wulff (1988) have outlined the basic steps involved in conducting SGID.

During the preinterview meeting the faculty member or faculty course director meets with the consultant, who may be an educational developer or a trained colleague, to discuss key course information and the data collection process. The teacher selects his or her preferred SGID feedback form, which typically includes two to three questions that lend themselves to consensus. Common questions are: "List the major strengths in the course: what is helping you learn? Please explain briefly, or give an example for each strength"; and, "List the changes you would make in the course to assist you in learning. Please explain how these suggested changes could be made." Each group of students responds to these questions on a single worksheet, as described later.

During the ensuing thirty- to forty-minute in-class interview, often conducted at midterm, the consultant introduces herself and explains the SGID process. Typically, students learn that its primary purpose is to strengthen course practices and procedures, rather than to focus on the individual instructor. They are assured that the SGID procedure is voluntary, anonymous, and confidential. No comments are attributed to any one student, and the instructor or course director receives a composite report containing representative comments.

The consultant then asks students to form groups of six to eight and select a recorder. The groups discuss the questions on the feedback form, and the student recorder writes down the points on which the group members reach consensus. After this eight- to twelve-minute process, the consultant records in turn the consensus-based comments of each group on a central chalkboard. A student recorder copies everything from the board so that there is a permanent record. (In our experience it is wise to check these notes for accuracy and completeness before erasing the board.) Whenever possible we have used a portable electronic board that allows us to capture a printout of all the data with the press of a button.

The consultant, whether peer or professional, has several key tasks. During the whole-class discussion following the group work, she asks students for clarification or amplification of ambiguous points, and seeks to determine whether there is general consensus on the issues raised. To accomplish the latter, she asks for a show of hands indicating agreement or disagreement with particular comments. We usually record these numbers next to the question (for example, "The exams should be multiple choice rather than essay," eleven agree, four disagree). We also consciously prompt students to word their comments as constructively as possible.

In the postclassroom phase of SGID, the consultant analyzes and organizes the material to make it meaningful to the instructor or the course director. The comments can be arranged, for example, in order of frequency under the headings "things to continue," "things to consider changing," and "other suggestions." It is helpful if the consultant can group responses under common themes. Not all comments are included verbatim, particularly ones with potentially hurtful phrasing, but representative remarks are useful to convey the flavor of the interview. As White (1991) points out, during the feedback sessions the consultant seeks to promote reflection on the issues prior to identifying strategies for change.

During the final phase of the process the instructor discusses the results of the interview with the students. Like the classroom assessment techniques advocated by Angelo and Cross (1993), the SGID procedure raises student expectations for positive change. Thus it is essential that faculty members offer students explanations of those course elements they are willing and able to address. Like many others, we have found that SGID offers an enormously positive way to strengthen teaching and also to foster, as Black (1998) notes, stronger bonds between students and faculty to promote successful teaching and learning.

Interactive Student Focus Groups

Focus groups are a common marketing tool used by corporations to gather data about new products, customer satisfaction, and a host of other issues. They tend to be action oriented in that clients will typically base decisions on data they feel are representative and reliable. Such groups involve highly paid professional moderators, expensive facilities (including one-way mirrors and sophisticated recording equipment), and complex data analysis that takes into account nonverbal as well as verbal responses. Focus groups conducted by professionals in higher education have frequently targeted recruiting and fund-raising issues. However, we have found that focus groups for courses or programs can be conducted effectively and efficiently by trained faculty peer consultants, who use a highly structured protocol developed at USAFA.

Like the other forms of consultation discussed here, focus groups involve a four-step process with a preinterview conference, the interview itself, the postinterview debriefing and, whenever possible, feedback to students. The preinterview conference is particularly important because the faculty member, often in concert with other department members, must provide a series of critical questions for students to address during the fifty-minute focus group session.

The consultant must review these questions with care and determine the most effective way to present them. Questions such as, "How much time did you devote to the course?" or, "Was the evaluation system fair?" are compiled into a one-page survey, which is given to students to complete when they first arrive. This allows the consultants to greet students personally and to get them started on a specific task. The activity also seems to put students at ease. Those who arrive late complete the survey afterward if they have time, but in fact it is not necessary to have everyone do the task.

The introductory remarks are similar to the comments made prior to conducting SGID. We also emphasize to students that their input will have an impact and that changes will occur. We assure anonymity by assigning each student a unique number to use while the interview is audiotaped. Students quickly catch on: "This is Number 2, and I disagree with Number 14 that we should have more field trips." The tapes are then transcribed by someone unfamiliar with the students' voices, so that the interview is captured without indications of either gender or individual identity. Students are asked to write their numbers on any materials before handing them back. Thus, if intriguing comments arise during the discussion, we have a way of correlating data points.

The other questions supplied by the faculty member are sorted into two types: open-ended questions, for which the consultant waits for volunteer respondents, and round-robin questions, to which everyone responds in turn. Responses to round-robin questions such as, "What is the most important thing you learned in this course?" are often of greatest value.

Usually we ask about ten questions, breaking them up at about the halfway point to conduct a ten-minute roundtable ranking activity. For this exercise students in small groups are asked to rapidly generate ideas—two minutes per topic—by passing a sheet of paper among themselves, with each student in turn adding an idea as he or she says it aloud. The students brainstorm first the strengths of the course and then the things about it they would change. Then, striving for consensus, they rank order the three most positive things about the class and then the three most important changes they would like to see. This activity, which also uses a worksheet with instructional prompts, is like a mini-SGID, but we do not ask students to report back to the whole class or for a whole-group consensus. The groups merely turn in their worksheets, noting their identifying numbers, for later compilation.

During the interview session itself we usually involve two consultants: one to conduct the activities and pose the questions using an overhead projector and the other to audiotape responses. Recording the sessions maximizes the data capture, but the equipment is seldom totally reliable. In our experience it is wise to have the second facilitator also jot down at least the opening words of each comment next to the student's number. This written record simplifies the later transcription because it gives the transcriber a road map. And in the event of an equipment failure much of the interview can be reconstructed.

After the interview is over, the second consultant, a professional transcribing company, or a trained support person with the proper equipment prepares a transcript. Once the data have been transcribed and analyzed, one or both of the consultants sits down with the faculty member, and if appropriate other department members, to discuss and interpret the findings and plan future changes.

A unique technique developed at USAFA is used with both focus groups and SGID. Students are asked to record on an index card two things: first, a single word or phrase that describes their perception of the course ("boring," "stimulating," "confusing," "as dry as eating saltines in the Sahara") and, second, a number from 1 (low) to 5 (high) to describe their satisfaction with the course. This index card activity serves several valuable functions. When the students quickly read off what they wrote, round-robin style, the consultants get an immediate sense of the group's attitude toward the course. Furthermore, this candid self-disclosure promotes an open, trusting atmosphere, one in which students don't have to second-guess each other's attitudes.

Quantitatively, because we often do SGID or focus groups in a series over time (both within a single unit of a course and over several years of a particular course), the numbers give a measurable mean for each course that can serve as a benchmark as changes are made. Recently, we began sharing the numbers and comments with instructors in a bar graph format (generated with Microsoft Excel). For example, a bar indicating eight students rated the course with a three would likely be taller than other bars and would contain the comments embedded in it for easy reference. In addition to the transcript with the questions, faculty members or course directors also receive written summaries of this index card activity, the student survey, and the roundtable ranking activity.

Focus groups are similar to SGID in that they involve consultants, whether peers or professionals, conducting structured student interviews. However, there are some key differences. For one thing, SGID is conducted in the classroom during class time, when there is a likelihood that large numbers of students will participate. Thus the sample size is large and representative. Focus groups usually rely on volunteers coming during non-class hours, so the sample is likely to be more biased—often with students who particularly like or dislike a course. However, because focus groups, particularly those targeting courses with multiple sections, often draw heterogeneous students from different classes, there is a greater opportunity for candid interactions outside the familiar peer relationships in ongoing classes. We encourage faculty to make the sample as random as possible. One effective technique involves drawing from a hat the names of several students in each section and specifically asking them to participate. Usually, because the drawing is public, the response is positive and the sample is more representative.

To eliminate the bias problem altogether, we have successfully used our focus group protocol (survey, index card activity, round-robin and voluntary questions, and the roundtable ranking activity) with entire courses. In an experimental core course for law, for example, all three sections met during their regular class time in a conference room equipped with microphones, overhead projector, and recording equipment. Because fifteen to sixteen students were involved in each class, we asked fewer round-robin and voluntary questions, but the rich data gathered enabled the law department to make key changes in its course structure and content, textbooks, and evaluation methods (Millis and Fitzkee, 1998).

Like Wright and Hendershott (1992), we have found focus groups to be an invaluable means of tapping student perceptions within a university setting. Interactions among students, particularly when the facilitators are able to probe responses, yield rich data that cannot be obtained from traditional surveys. Furthermore, as Popham (1993) notes, the participants' synergy provides a stimulating environment for collecting rich data. We often conclude a focus group by asking about the process itself. Comments are unfailingly positive: "Someone is finally listening to us"; "I wasn't sure what to expect, but this experience was really positive."

Classroom Observations

At USAFA, classroom observations are routinely conducted at the departmental level by peers. We have an open-door policy, highly unusual in academia, which evolved naturally as part of the Air Force performance review process and as a proactive response to the large number of junior officers entering classrooms at the M.A. degree level and without college or university teaching experience. Such officers remain at the Academy for three years or less, although many return on subsequent tours, so getting them up to speed as rapidly as possible is a matter of ethical responsibility and institutional commitment.

The nineteen departments organize and conduct peer observations in ways that reflect their disciplinary priorities. One quantitatively based department, for example, has a public display board that tracks the systematically scheduled observations, listing and checking off who visits whom and when. In a humanities department, course directors are expected to visit the classes of all those teaching the course for which they are responsible, but scheduling and feedback are purely private, often loosely conducted matters.

The purpose of observations and the feedback process is equally diverse. Some departments are careful to identify observers out of the chain of command who offer confidential, formative evaluation. In other departments, evaluative comments are shared with supervisors or become documents available to departmental colleagues with a need to know, such as those who are on the committee to select the department's Outstanding Academy Educator. Many departments have developed highly sophisticated feedback forms based on literature surveys and departmental expectations. Other departments are equally committed to classroom observations but prefer more informal procedures.

Given this open-door climate, the CEE plays a service-oriented role. We observe classes at the request of individuals or departments, often augmented by videotaping, and we offer training workshops on conducting effective classroom observations at the institutional and departmental levels.

When we videotape, we usually work with two consultants. One consultant typically operates two cameras, one focused at the front of the classroom where most teachers stand and the other panning the classroom for student reactions. The second consultant sits among the students, usually out of camera range to capture other student reactions. After the observation the instructor receives the videotape for private review, and then the two consultants look at the tape and the observer's notes and prepare for an in-depth feedback session. The faculty member and consultants meet and have the tape available for viewing segments that relate to particular teaching concerns. We agree with Keig and Waggoner (1994) that videotaping can be a powerful catalyst for promoting change. In general the discussion focuses on possible teaching improvements, rather than reviewing the entire tape.

The workshops I developed to train consultants in classroom observation (Millis, 1989; 1992; 1994) are based on the premise that such observations should be conducted in a positive atmosphere. Even on campuses where peer review is mandatory, faculty should strive to build collegiality. There are no excuses for bypassing opportunities to help other colleagues.

Rather than a single visit that results in a quick but isolated snapshot, class observations are most effective when they are part of an ongoing series. Several researchers (Wilkerson, 1988; Weimer, 1990) recommend a collaborative, reciprocal approach in which the professional status of both parties is respected and celebrated. Reciprocal observations (peer-to-peer) virtually guarantee the positive approach essential for constructive change. This reciprocity should also include the students, who are key players in the process. Teachers should inform them of the nature and purpose of the visit, introduce them to the visitor(s), and encourage them to welcome the consultants into the classroom.

The preobservation meeting is extremely important. Here teacher and consultant discuss obvious things such as course objectives and teaching methods. Other topics, often overlooked, are also important. Instructors should identify areas of their teaching on which they particularly want feedback (transitions between topics, pacing, relevance of anecdotes, for example) and anything special about the class, such as exceptionally motivated students, a disruptive clique sitting in the back, or poor room design.

They can also explore the role played by the consultant. In a visit to an English class, for example, a consultant in the same discipline might serve as a group member as students critique their peers' papers. Such involvement would give her more insights into student learning and teacher facilitation than would remaining in the back of the room. Similarly, the consultant should know how to respond to unsolicited student input, such as, "I just want you to know that Teacher X is wonderful [or terrible]." Some faculty members welcome such student self-disclosure even though it is highly selective. Others might prefer that the consultant discourage the conversation with a courteous comment, such as, "I really appreciate your insights, but Professor X and I agreed that my visit would focus on objective observations." The faculty member and the consultant should also set up in advance the means and place for sharing feedback and its nature, whether oral or written. "Sooner is better" is a good rule for scheduling the debriefing session.

During the visit the consultant should attempt to capture holistically what is occurring in the classroom, keeping in mind the particular aspects of teaching and learning identified by the instructor during the preobservation conference. Many observers use a notepad to record a virtual transcript of what unfolds; in the margin they note comments for the instructor, such as, "Three students left the room," or, "Ten students raised their hands." If specific feedback forms are used, they should not be completed on the spot. Reflective, insightful commentary is essential.

The feedback session is critically important. In the case of a voluntary visit, often the feedback is oral rather than written. In some institutions written feedback may be required, or faculty members may request it so they can include it in a professional portfolio. A number of observation instruments are available to guide this process. On the whole, focused narratives (Lewis, 1997; Chism, 1999) are preferable to checklists, which do not capture the subtleties of classroom teaching and learning.

Whether oral or written, the feedback should be accurate and provide an objective record of the behaviors and activities recorded. It should be honest, offering information that may at times be painful for the instructor. At the same time feedback should be phrased positively, with an emphasis on observed behaviors rather than judgmental interpretations. Often a questioning technique, accompanied with direct suggestions, can accompany the factual data: "As my notes suggest, two of the three groups I sat with were engaged in off-task behaviors such as discussing a movie or wondering if you would postpone the midterm because of my visit. Have you ever tried monitoring the groups, much as I did? Or giving them an extension activity— an extra task to complete—if they have finished the initial one? Assigning student roles, such as group leader and timekeeper, can help students become more responsible for the activities within groups."

The feedback should be context specific and concrete so that the instructor knows exactly when given behaviors occurred. For example, a consultant observing an American history class might note, "Following your rapid explanation of the six causes of the Civil War, the students seated near me had puzzled expressions as they thumbed through their handout and squinted at the board jammed with notes." The discussion should also be action oriented, with an emphasis on presenting the data, interpreting the observations, and making plans to strengthen the learning in the class.

Successful classroom observations should accomplish at least two goals. They should reinforce positive behaviors (things that the instructor is doing right), and they should lead to changes in behaviors to improve teaching (things the instructor could improve). Thus a skilled observer will both offer information and provide inspiration. Based on the results of the consultation, the instructor should not only know what to change but also be motivated to expend the necessary effort to do so. It is helpful to record teaching improvement ideas—a sort of teaching action plan that emerges from the postvisit discussion. Subsequent classroom observations to evaluate the effectiveness of the changes will ensure a process of continuous improvement.

Conclusions

We are fortunate that collegiality and networking routinely occur in the faculty development world. Fellow practitioners share ideas and insights through national and international organizations, and such collegial sharing can also be encouraged within campuses. As individuals, departments, and institutions become more accountable, faculty members are becoming increasingly involved with self- and peer assessment of teaching. Involving faculty members as peer consultants not only opens classroom doors, but also stimulates conversations about the teaching and learning process.

References

Angelo, T. A., and Cross, K. P. *Classroom Assessment Techniques: A Handbook for College Teachers.* (2nd ed.) San Francisco: Jossey-Bass, 1993.
Black, B. "Using the SGID Method for a Variety of Purposes." *To Improve the Academy,* 1998, *17,* 245–262.

Chism, N.V.N. *Peer Review of Teaching: A Sourcebook.* Bolton, Mass.: Anker, 1999.

Clark, D., and Redmond, M. *Small Group Instructional Diagnosis: Final Report,* 1982. (ED 217 954)

Diamond, N. A. "S.G.I.D. (Small Group Instructional Diagnosis): Tapping Student Perceptions of Teaching." In E. C. Wadsworth (ed.), *A Handbook for New Practitioners.* Stillwater, Okla.: New Forums Press/Professional and Organizational Development Network in Higher Education, 1988.

Keig, L., and Waggoner, M. D. *Collaborative Peer Review: The Role of Faculty in Improving College Teaching.* ASHE-ERIC Higher Education Report No. 2. Washington, D.C.: The George Washington University School of Education and Human Development, 1994.

Lewis, K. "Collecting Information Using Class Observation." In K. T. Brinko and R. J. Menges (eds.), *Practically Speaking: A Sourcebook for Instructional Consultants in Higher Education.* Stillwater, Okla.: New Forums Press, 1997.

Millis, B. J. "Colleagues Helping Colleagues: A Peer Observation Program Model." *Journal of Staff, Program, and Organization Development,* 1989, *7,* 15–21.

Millis, B. J. "Conducting Effective Peer Classroom Observations." *To Improve the Academy,* 1992, *11,* 189–206.

Millis, B. J. "Forging the Ties That Bind: Peer Mentoring Part-Time Faculty." In M. A. Wunsch (ed.), *Mentoring Revisited: Making an Impact on Individuals and Institutions.* New Directions for Teaching and Learning, no. 57. San Francisco: Jossey-Bass, 1994.

Millis, B. J., and Fitzkee, D. "Using Interactive Focus Groups to Assess Programs and Courses." Presentation at the American Association of Higher Education National conference, Atlanta, 1998.

Nyquist, J. D., and Wulff, D. H. "Consultation Using a Research Perspective." In E. C. Wadsworth (ed.), *A Handbook for New Practitioners.* Stillwater, Okla.: New Forums Press/Professional and Organizational Development Network in Higher Education, 1988.

Popham, J. *Educational Evaluation.* (3rd ed.) Boston: Allyn & Bacon, 1993.

Weimer, M. *Improving College Teaching: Strategies for Developing Instructional Effectiveness.* San Francisco: Jossey-Bass, 1990.

White, K. "Small Group Instructional Diagnosis: Alternate Adult Assessment." *Adult Assessment Forum,* 1991, *1* (3), 6–7, 10.

Wilkerson, L. "Classroom Observation: The Observer as Collaborator." In E. C. Wadsworth (ed.), *A Handbook for New Practitioners.* Stillwater, Okla.: New Forums Press/Professional and Organizational Development Network in Higher Education, 1988.

Wright, S. P., and Hendershott, A. "Using Focus Groups to Obtain Students' Perceptions of General Education." *To Improve the Academy,* 1992, *11,* 87–104.

BARBARA J. MILLIS *is director of faculty development at the United States Air Force Academy.*

4

A systemwide instructional consultation program involves full-time faculty serving as instructional consultants to their colleagues.

Instructional Consultation in a Statewide Setting

Michael A. Kerwin

The Teaching Consultation Program offered in the University of Kentucky Community College System (UKCCS) provides faculty members an opportunity to analyze their teaching behavior and to work with a colleague acting as a consultant to make changes. Faculty members who provide this consulting service come from each of the thirteen geographically dispersed community colleges in the system. Each of these individuals teaches full-time and has been recognized by his or her college president as an outstanding teacher. Each has attended a two-day workshop on instructional consultation and is reassigned from one three-credit class to work with two colleagues each teaching term. Each college has more than one consultant, and during a particular term two or more will often be working with four or more of their colleagues. During a typical academic term, fifteen consultants at thirteen different colleges work with thirty colleagues. Since the program was introduced in 1977, more than seven hundred faculty members have participated as consultants or as teachers.

The Teaching Consultation Program was inspired by the program developed in the School of Education at the University of Massachusetts at Amherst in the early 1970s, but differs significantly from this model. As in the University of Massachusetts approach (described by Bergquist and Phillips, 1977), the Teaching Consultation Program is designed to help faculty recognize and consciously develop instructional behaviors most appropriate for themselves and their students. Faculty members volunteer to participate, and none of the data collected are used for evaluation purposes. The program, like its model, has six phases: initial contact, initial interview, data collection, data review and analysis, planning and implementing

NEW DIRECTIONS FOR TEACHING AND LEARNING, no. 79, Fall 1999 © Jossey-Bass Publishers changes, and evaluation. A modified version of the Teaching Analysis by Students (TABS) questionnaire, developed at the University of California at Berkeley, is used to collect information from students about teaching behavior. Data are collected using multiple methods: interviewing the teacher, observing the class, videotaping the teacher, and surveying the students.

There are two significant features of the Teaching Consultation Program that differ from the University of Massachusetts model. First, full-time faculty serve as consultants. In the University of Massachusetts approach, educational specialists serve as consultants. Second, each semester all consultants attend a systemwide workshop during the data review and analysis phase of the program and present formal descriptions of the teachers with whom they are working to the other consultants in the system.

These two features—the use of full-time teachers as instructional consultants and the systemwide consultant workshops—have contributed significantly to the longevity, popularity, and effectiveness of the Teaching Consultation Program in the UKCCS. Implementation, maintenance, and development of the program in a statewide system of community colleges has also required coordination and support on a system level.

This chapter describes the key elements of the UKCCS program, including program implementation, selection and preparation of consultants, program coordination, professional development for consultants, administrative support, and program evaluation. Because these topics are so interrelated with the program itself, however, the perspectives of faculty and consultants provide a useful introduction. The following scenario is designed to illustrate briefly what typically occurs in each of the six phases of the program.

The Faculty Perspective

Asked to describe the Teaching Consultation Program, a participating faculty member might make this report about the experience.

Initial Interest

I became interested in the Teaching Consultation Program after hearing about it from a colleague. After teaching at the college for several years, I wanted to make a few changes in my teaching. To be more specific, I wanted my students to become more actively involved in the class. Being untenured, however, I was concerned about doing something that might fail, lead to poor student evaluations, and affect my promotion possibilities. I didn't want to risk a poor evaluation. I heard that the instructional consultant at my college would help me to identify what I might do and help me implement the changes in a confidential way. I contacted her and arranged a meeting to discuss my concerns and goals.

Initial Interview

I met with the consultant who clarified the confidential nature of our relationship and explained the process. I agreed to participate and to allow myself to be videotaped. We decided to focus on one class, and the consultant began collecting data about that class, such as my syllabus, examinations, and assignments. We set a date for her to observe my teaching and another date for her to videotape the class. We also set a regular time for weekly meetings.

Data Collection

During our next three meetings the consultant and I continued to discuss my class and my teaching goals. During the fifth week of the semester, on her third visit to my class, she administered a student questionnaire that focused on my teaching behavior. I also completed the questionnaire, predicting how the students would rate me on each of the items. By this time I had also seen the videotape and identified a few changes that I wanted to make in the way I teach. I had a tendency to put my left hand into my pocket, for example. I felt this behavior distracted the students from my lectures.

Data Review and Analysis

The consultant and I reviewed all of the data she had collected. We identified three of my teaching strengths and three areas that could be changed. I had not realized that students were confused somewhat about the major and minor points of my lectures.

Planning and Implementing Changes

I focused on four specific changes that I wanted to make in my class and the consultant helped me to identify strategies for making these changes. To clarify important themes, for example, I would ask students to write a one-minute paper at the end of class, identifying the major point of the day's lecture. I would then discuss what they had written at the beginning of the next class. The consultant and I discussed my progress at our weekly meetings. I realized that to achieve a high level of active student involvement, I would have to change some of my teaching on the first day of class. Nevertheless, I felt I had made some progress.

Evaluation

During the final three weeks of the semester the consultant evaluated my success in achieving my goals for change. She made another classroom visit, videotaped my class a second time, and administered another student questionnaire. The videotape showed that I no longer had my left hand in my pocket, and the questionnaire indicated that students thought they were more involved in the class. Nevertheless, I believed I could do better. Overall, I felt good about the experience and expressed my satisfaction on the evaluation form that I completed and sent to the systemwide coordinator.

The Consultant Perspective

If the consultant in the scenario above were to describe her experience, the narrative might include the following notes.

Initial Interest

The professor called me to discuss his interest in participating in the Teaching Consultation Program. Although I was enthusiastic about working with him, I was concerned about my lack of knowledge in his teaching area. I wondered if he really wished to make changes in his teaching or mainly wanted to use the experience to strengthen his argument for promotion to associate professor.

Initial Interview

The teacher convinced me that in fact he wanted to change his teaching to enable students to learn more effectively. He was an extremely organized teacher and spent many hours preparing for his lectures. I wondered if he could shift the focus from transmitting knowledge to facilitating student learning.

Data Collection

His lectures were interesting, but I was concerned about how I could help him.

Data Review and Analysis

I attended the Teaching Consultants Workshop and gave a formal presentation about the teacher to a group of other consultants, including two who taught in the same discipline. I began with a three-minute introduction, followed by a ten-minute videotape of the teacher at work. In the ensuing discussion the other consultants identified some excellent strategies for working with the teacher and helping him to achieve his goals.

Planning and Implementing Changes

After attending the workshop I felt well prepared for our planning sessions. Although I anticipated most of what he would want to do, I was surprised about the hand-in-the-pocket concern. Nevertheless, if that was a change that he wanted to make, I would help him achieve it.

Evaluation

The videotape and the student questionnaires showed that the teacher had indeed changed. By working with him I also learned some strategies that I would like to try in one of my own classes. I enjoyed the consultation and hoped that we could continue to get together occasionally to chat about our teaching experiences.

Elements in the Systemwide Structure

As described above, both the consultant and the faculty member benefited from their experiences in the Teaching Consultation Program; the experiences of each, however, differed somewhat. In the initial phases of the program, for example, the instructor was concerned that data collected might be used in the evaluation of his teaching; the consultant was concerned about the teacher's motivation for change. In the data collection phase, the consultant and the teacher noticed different things. For example, the teacher was concerned about having his hand in his pocket; the consultant saw him as being an effective lecturer whose style differed from that of other teachers she had observed. She wondered if she could identify teaching strategies that would be appropriate for him.

The systemwide workshop enabled the consultant to discuss her concerns about working with the teacher with other consultants, including two who taught in his discipline, and receive feedback and suggestions about teaching strategies that he might consider using. After the workshop, the consultant returned to the college with a number of strategies that she could discuss with her colleague. In addition, she now knew other consultants whom she could call to discuss future concerns if they arose.

The systemwide structure of the Teaching Consultation Program was designed, therefore, to support the ongoing efforts of all faculty—consultants and teachers—to recognize and consciously develop instructional behaviors most appropriate for themselves and their students.

The Initial Phase. Elements in the initial phases of program development included establishing policies, coordinating program development, preparing and selecting consultants, and providing necessary funding for program operation.

Establishing Policies. To implement the Teaching Consultation Program on a systemwide basis, the following policies were developed, implemented, and maintained: (1) providing incentives for consultants to participate, (2) giving consultants the freedom to determine with whom they would consult, and (3) separating the program from the evaluation process.

Incentives were a primary concern. In the UKCCS, each instructional consultant was excused from teaching one three-credit class in order to work with two colleagues during each academic term. Time was more than an incentive in the system: it was a need, because the normal teaching load was fifteen credit hours each semester. The consultant's need for consulting time can be illustrated by an actual incident.

As a part of the program the faculty member completes an evaluation form at the end of the semester and sends it to the systemwide coordinator. Ninety-eight percent of the comments on these evaluation forms are positive. In this case, however, a faculty member submitted an evaluation form praising the program and describing how much it had helped her, but she added that she wished that she could have spent more time with the consultant. The coordinator was surprised to read about the faculty member's concern: her consultant was a veteran who was regarded as one of the most effective in the system. The coordinator, fearing that the consultant had become ill or been injured, contacted the consultant and learned that she had taught a full load of courses that semester. As dedicated as she was, she had been unable to teach a full load and devote enough time to the faculty member requesting help.

Giving consultants the freedom to decide with whom they will consult was another policy decision. It was realized that working with faculty members who participated just because their department chair told them to do so would be a waste of the consultant's time. For change to occur the teacher has to be internally motivated.

Finally, the program was separated from the evaluation process so that faculty felt free to take risks. By keeping evaluation separate, faculty were also more willing to volunteer to participate and to help achieve the goal of creating a learning community in which all faculty analyzed their teaching and made changes to help students learn more effectively.

Partly for that reason, instructional consultants serving as division chairs or academic deans could not participate as consultants in the program while in those roles. At the same time, developing and implementing these policies required cooperation from senior-level administrators. This was a crucial element in the initial phases of program development. Senior-level administrators had to understand that the program was not *remedial;* it was designed to help good faculty become better. Administrators also had to accept that it would be a program controlled by faculty.

Coordinating Program Development. Another crucial element in the initial phase of program development was providing program coordination. Typically, one of the single most important factors in implementing an instructional consultation program is the determination of an individual, sometimes a faculty member, at other times a senior administrator, to do so (Kerwin, 1997).

In the UKCCS, about one-fifth of the time of the systemwide faculty development coordinator's time was allocated to the Teaching Consultation Program. Initially, this coordination involved designing a procedure for selecting and preparing faculty members to be consultants and implementing and evaluating a pilot project. Coordination also included the preparation of computer printouts of results of student questionnaires that were administered as part of the program.

Selecting and Preparing Consultants. Enabling the college presidents to nominate instructional consultants was one of the trade-offs for their support. The systemwide coordinator contacted all nominees, discussed the program with them, and recommended willing candidates to the chancellor, who invited those recommended to attend the introductory two-day workshop.

Another key element in the initial phase of program development was preparing consultants to implement the program. To accomplish this, over two days at the beginning of the semester, consultants attended the sixteen-hour workshop mentioned earlier, led by veteran instructional consultants. Each of the faculty who attended the workshop also received a three-ring binder that included all workshop materials and resources needed to conduct the program. Instead of returning immediately to their college to recruit faculty consultees, consultants in the new program worked together as consultants and teachers during the first teaching term. The recruiting issue was postponed until the next semester.

Funding. Materials must be available for consultants to do their work. Hence promotional brochures and student questionnaires were designed and printed. Opscan sheets were purchased and computer support for analyzing student questionnaires was provided. All of these needs required financial support, which was borne by the system office. However, the most significant costs were borne by the colleges. With the chancellor's support, college presidents reassigned each instructional consultant from one three-credit class to consult each semester. They also provided the funding for consultants to attend the systemwide workshops.

The Operational Phase. In the operational phase the elements included coordinating the program, providing for the professional development of consultants, preparing new consultants, evaluating the program, and making appropriate changes. These issues were hidden in the scenario described earlier but were necessary to support it.

Coordinating the Program. Once the program was implemented, two of the most important systemwide functions were to develop a calendar for the program and to coordinate the systemwide workshop planned for each semester. The structure of the University of Massachusetts model facilitated the process of developing a calendar. Consultants were expected to complete the initial phases of the program, including data collection, in the first five weeks of the semester. The systemwide workshop, which was designed to enable the consultants to synthesize all data collected and present these findings to other consultants, was planned to occur in the sixth week of each semester. To prepare for their presentations, consultants had to administer the TABS questionnaire to their teachers' classes and have the data tabulated in an interpretable format.

This tabulation was done by the system office. At the end of the fifth week consultants submitted the Opscan sheets completed by students and teachers for scanning and conversion into computer files. A software program generated a printout that consultants could use to interpret the evaluation data when they gave their workshop presentations. Copies were made available to both consultant and faculty member.

The systemwide workshop began at one o'clock on a Thursday afternoon and ended at noon on Friday. (A more detailed description of the workshop is presented by Kerwin and Rhoads, 1993.) This schedule enabled consultants to travel to and from the workshop site but did not allow time for each consultant to attend all of the presentations. Instead, most of the workshop time was allocated to concurrent sessions, with three or four consultant presentations occurring simultaneously. The coordinator scheduled these presentations so that no two concurrent presentations concerned teachers from the same discipline. In each presentation, a consultant showed a videotape of a teacher and discussed that teacher with other consultants, and this scheduling enabled presenting consultants to receive helpful advice from consultants in the teacher's discipline. If a consultant who taught English was working with a nursing instructor, for example, having nursing faculty-consultants in the session was helpful.

Professional Development of Consultants. The initial two-day workshop served as only minimal preparation to be a teaching consultant, even for faculty who were recognized as being outstanding teachers. But attending the ongoing consultants' workshops each semester and analyzing eight to ten case studies at each workshop greatly enhanced consultants' knowledge and skill. To provide further professional development consultants were encouraged to attend sessions at appropriate conferences, such as the annual meeting of the Professional and Organizational Network in Higher Education.

In addition, two UKCCS workshops targeted toward teaching consultants were held each academic year. Nationally recognized experts presented the workshops in Kentucky, and instructional consultants were reimbursed for their in-state travel expenses. Sometimes these workshops were delivered to multiple sites using the university's Interactive Television Network. Topics in this workshop series have included small group instructional diagnosis, classroom research, mastery learning, solving problems of small group teaching, and using videotapes in consultation.

Preparing New Consultants. Between 1983 and 1998, ninety full-time faculty served as instructional consultants. Fifty-eight (65 percent) were women and thirty-two (36 percent) were men. Of these, twenty (22 percent) represented technical programs (accounting, business, computer information systems, clinical laboratory technician, education, human services, nursing, and office administration), and seventy (78 percent) represented general education programs (such as art, English, and mathematics). Although fifty-five (61 percent) served for six to fifteen years as teaching consultants, sixteen (18 percent) served for one year or less. Reasons for discontinuing service included being appointed to an administrative position, resigning to accept a job outside the system, and retirement. Obviously, a procedure was needed for preparing new consultants, assuring that they represented a wide variety of disciplines and were available at each college.

This was accomplished by monitoring the availability of potential consultants and arranging for the two-day new consultant training workshops on an as-needed basis—usually every two years. Just as in the initial phase, college presidents were asked to nominate potential consultants.

In 1999, thirty-eight of the full-time faculty served as consultants. Their characteristics were similar to those seen in the group over time. Twenty-eight (74 percent) were women; ten (26 percent) were men. Nineteen (50 percent) had appointments as English or communication faculty. Nine (24 percent) represented technical areas, and 29 (76 percent) represented general education areas.

Evaluating the Program. Program evaluation was another important systemwide concern. From an institutional standpoint, senior administrators wanted to know that their expenditures were worth the investment. As

Robert Menges (1996) has pointed out, research is badly needed in this area. Erickson (1997) also noted that evaluation could increase a program's credibility, enhance the competence of the consultants, and ensure program survival.

The first systematic study in the UKCCS was conducted in 1988–89. It showed the program was effective in helping faculty to change their student-perceived teaching behavior, that these changes were seen by students in classes other than those targeted in the Teaching Consultation Program, and that they persisted over time (Rozeman and Kerwin, 1991). Significantly, student ratings for participating teachers rose by a full point on a five-point scale. The results of this study were disseminated widely in the system.

In addition, the system was fortunate to have an external consultant evaluate its program. Diane Morrison (1995), a faculty development specialist from British Columbia, studied the Teaching Consultation Program as part of her dissertation research. In her study she cited the program as the most comprehensive of the programs that she examined and that were targeted at individual faculty.

Implementing Changes. As described earlier, the core of the systemwide Teaching Consultation Program was consultant-faculty interaction. Program change required the participation of the consultants, and if consultants felt that a change could improve their effectiveness, the systemwide coordinator convened an ad hoc planning committee to discuss the idea and to recommend a course of action. It was through this process that the TABS questionnaire was revised to have a lower reading level and less ambiguous statements. A pilot program was also implemented at several local high schools, and many consultants began using small group instructional diagnosis to supplement data collected from students on the TABS.

Conclusion

This chapter has outlined the key elements of an instructional consultation program in a statewide system of community colleges in which full-time faculty serve as consultants to their colleagues. Self-perceptions of both faculty and consultants changed as they went through the six phases of the program. Teachers became more aware of their teaching behavior and its effect on students; consultants learned new teaching strategies that they could use themselves as well as in advising faculty.

The chapter also described several key administrative and organizational elements that supported this interaction on the statewide level. Such elements included systemwide policies, regular workshops, and mechanisms for program coordination, computer support, and program evaluation. As the consultants and the faculty members proceeded through each phase of the program, the systemwide coordinator worked with the college presidents and the system chancellor to ensure that the program was available to all faculty, that the appropriate faculty were selected to become consultants, and that the consultants were prepared to conduct the program. The coordinator also worked with teaching consultants and faculty to monitor the effectiveness of the program and to make appropriate changes in the program itself.

In short, a well-organized instructional consultation program, with support from faculty, staff, and administration, can make a difference in the quality of teaching not just at the individual level but across an entire statewide system of community colleges.

References

Bergquist, W. H., and Phillips, S. R. *A Handbook for Faculty Development.* Vol. 2. Washington, D.C.: Council for the Advancement of Small Colleges, 1977.

Erickson, G. R. "Issues in Evaluating Consultation." In K. T. Brinko and R. J. Menges (eds.), *Practically Speaking: A Sourcebook for Instructional Consultation in Higher Education.* Stillwater, Okla.: New Forums Press, 1997.

Kerwin, M. A. "Considerations in Setting Up an Instructional Consultation Program." In K. T. Brinko and R. J. Menges (eds.), *Practically Speaking: A Sourcebook for Instructional Consultation in Higher Education.* Stillwater, Okla.: New Forums Press, 1997.

Kerwin, M. A., and Rhoads, J. "The Teaching Consultants' Workshop." *To Improve the Academy,* 1993, *12,* 69–77.

Menges, R. J. "Instructional Consultation in Higher Education: Past, Present, and Future." Paper presented at the annual conference of the Professional and Organizational Network in Higher Education, Salt Lake City, Utah, Oct. 1996.

Morrison, D. E. "Opening Doors to Better Teaching: The Role of Peer-Based Instructional Consultation." Unpublished doctoral dissertation, Claremont Graduate School, 1995.

Rozeman, J. E., and Kerwin, M. A. "Evaluating the Effectiveness of a Teaching Consultation Program on Changing Student Ratings of Teacher Behaviors." *Journal of Staff, Program and Organization Development,* 1991, *9* (4), 223–230.

MICHAEL A. KERWIN *is the coordinator of Faculty, Staff, and Program Development for the University of Kentucky Community College System.*

5

*Faculty learning communities can facilitate peer consul-
tation and broaden the scope of its impact on individuals
and institutions.*

Peer Consultation and Faculty Learning Communities

Milton D. Cox

Consultation to improve teaching has traditionally been one-on-one. The individual instructor seeks advice from a consultant—usually an instructional developer in a confidential setting—about a teaching concern or initiative, then the instructor addresses the problem or opportunity and makes constructive changes. The outcome of this consultation, which may involve one or several meetings, is improved teaching and learning for the instructor and his or her students.

This chapter introduces a different model and describes ways that faculty learning communities can use peer consulting to broaden the scope of consultation and its impact on the individual and institution. As in individual consultation, many faculty reach out to join these communities because of a specific teaching concern or opportunity. But there may be more general or subtle reasons, sometimes unknown to the teacher, to join with a community of colleagues. Once they are part of such a group, teachers often discover other needs and opportunities that the learning community can help fulfill: offering empathy and encouragement, suggesting strategies, and catalyzing action.

For example, a junior faculty member seeking ways to improve student evaluation ratings may discover, after listening and sharing in the safety of a junior learning community, that there is a need to acknowledge and address the isolation and stress brought about by conflicting pressures of academic and personal life. Or a senior faculty member wanting to freshen up a familiar course may discover a new area of teaching or research while attending a national interdisciplinary conference with colleagues from the group.

If continued at an institution over several years, faculty learning communities can build a sense of collegiality around teaching and enhance the teaching and learning culture of the campus. Such communities can also create a cadre of faculty consultants willing to share their expertise with colleagues across the institution.

I have been developing and coordinating faculty learning communities for twenty years, and in this chapter I present successful examples, with a particular emphasis on peer consultation. With thoughtful planning and faculty and administrative support, these communities can be replicated on just about any campus. I indicate the concerns that faculty bring to these programs, the manner in which peer consulting takes place, and the outcomes for individual participants and the campus as a whole. Finally, I present recommendations for initiating and directing faculty learning communities that include peer consultation as an effective component.

What Are Faculty Learning Communities?

The concept of the learning community was born in the 1920s and 1930s with the work of Alexander Meiklejohn and John Dewey. Both were concerned about increasing specialization and fragmentation in higher education. Meiklejohn (1932) called for community of study and unity and coherence of curriculum across disciplines. Dewey (1933) advocated learning that was active, student centered, and involved shared inquiry. Coming to fruition in the 1980s, the combination of these approaches has produced a pedagogy and structure that has led, among other things, to increased student retention and intellectual development (Gabelnick, MacGregor, Matthews, and Smith, 1990).

The term *learning community* has traditionally been applied to programs that involve first- and second-year undergraduates, along with faculty who design the curriculum and teach the courses for such programs. I will call these traditional learning communities *student learning communities*, while keeping in mind that faculty play a key role. Indeed, good faculty development takes place in such situations through modeling, mentoring, and learning (Gabelnick, MacGregor, Matthews, and Smith, 1990).

In the context of this chapter I define a *faculty learning community* as a cross-disciplinary group of ten or so teachers who engage in an extended (typically yearlong) planned program to enhance teaching and learning and which incorporates frequent activities to facilitate learning, development, and community building. In fact student and faculty learning communities have many features in common. For example, Gabelnick and colleagues (1990, p. 69) comment that "the discussion and teamwork in learning communities compels students to discover what their fellow students bring to the material and how and what they think about it." The same is true for faculty colleagues.

A few faculty learning communities have existed since the beginning of the faculty development movement in the 1970s. For example, in the United States the Lilly Endowment's postdoctoral teaching awards program provides funding for research universities to establish groups of junior faculty that focus on teaching (Austin, 1992). However, these groups have generally not used the term learning communities or received much attention from faculty developers. For example, when Wright and O'Neil (1995) surveyed key instructional developers in the United States, Canada, the United Kingdom, and Australasia, there was no mention of faculty learning communities in the list of thirty-six development strategies. The predominant focus of most educational developers continues to be on one-on-one consultation employing eclectic strategies and techniques to meet the needs of the individual teacher (Tiberius, 1995).

Since the mid-1990s, however, interest in faculty learning communities has begun to grow. For example, Taylor (1997) examined research done at two large Australian universities on the way academics respond to pressures to adopt more flexible teaching practices. Four themes emerged from the research—tribalism, community, refuge (for safety), and the value of guiding principles for new practice; from these Taylor suggests five principles that might underlie the creation of faculty learning communities. They include time to do intensive learning, opportunities for *cross-tribal* conversation and collaboration about teaching, probing of belief systems and evaluation of teaching practices, refuges in which to explore new practices, and organizational support for these endeavors. In the following section, I give some examples of successful faculty learning communities that incorporate these principles, especially with respect to peer consultation.

Examples of Faculty Learning Communities

Faculty learning communities fall into two main categories: cohort-focused and issue-focused. I provide examples in each category. In each case the community in question is directed by Miami University's Teaching Effectiveness Programs and funded by Miami alumni through the Provost's Office. Each is advised by the Committee on the Enhancement of Learning and Teaching, which includes both faculty and students.

Cohort-focused learning communities are designed to address the teaching, learning, and developmental needs of an important cohort of faculty that has been particularly affected by the isolation, fragmentation, or chilly climate in the academy. The curriculum of such a community is shaped by the participants to include a broad range of teaching and learning areas and topics of interest to members. These communities can have an important impact on the culture of the institution if given long-term support. Two examples of cohort-focused communities at Miami are the Teaching Scholars Program, which provides peer consultation for junior faculty, and the Senior Faculty Program for Teaching Excellence, which is designed to provide the same for midcareer and senior professors.

Issue-focused learning communities address a special campus teaching and learning issue, such as diversity, technology, or peer evaluation of teaching. These groups offer membership across all faculty ranks and cohorts but with a focus on a particular theme. These communities are usually short-term, lasting about three years or until the issue of concern has been satisfactorily addressed. Two examples at Miami are the Faculty Group Using Difference to Enhance Teaching and Learning and the Teaching Portfolio Project.

Cohort-Focused Faculty Learning Communities. Junior faculty are one of the most important yet neglected resources for colleges and universities (Boice, 1992). They are often isolated from peers in other departments and ignored in campuswide efforts to change institutional culture. Although they report that many aspects of their careers are satisfying, junior faculty experience much stress in moving from their first year through to tenure (Sorcinelli, 1992). Most (90 to 95 percent) engage in defensive teaching practices, concentrate mostly on covering content, and are uncomfortable interacting with students (Boice, 1992). At Miami, the Teaching Scholars Program (Cox, 1994, 1995), which I have directed for twenty years, is designed to address these issues.

For the university the junior faculty learning community has the goals of increasing interest in undergraduate teaching and learning, broadening the evaluation of teaching and the assessment of learning, nourishing the scholarship of teaching, and encouraging faculty collaboration and reflection about general education and coherence of learning across disciplines (Cox, 1998). For the participants the objectives are to acquire information on teaching and learning through opportunities to observe, assess, and practice innovative teaching and uses of technology. The program provides time and financial support for individual investigations of teaching and learning problems and projects with the aim of having faculty develop thoughtful syllabi and clear learning objectives, and strengthening basic teaching skills. The latter might include, for example, leading class discussions, balancing lectures with active learning, communicating clearly with students, and devising meaningful tests and other assessment methods that achieve stated course objectives. Participants are offered help with investigation and incorporation of ways that difference can enhance teaching and learning, as well as means to undertake both formative and summative evaluation of instruction. There are opportunities to share ideas and advice with faculty mentors (current and former teaching scholars) and student consultants in order to develop awareness of teaching as an intellectual pursuit and to explore ways to engage in the scholarship of teaching. Finally, the learning community offers participants the chance to share their enthusiasm and experiences with other new faculty.

The junior faculty program is yearlong and involves around ten people. They attend biweekly seminars on topics selected by members of the community, take part in national teaching conferences and occasional all-day or overnight retreats, carry out individual teaching projects, and interact regularly with experienced faculty mentors and student consultants selected by the participants. Each participant receives release time from one course, funds for his or her teaching project, and conference expenses. Participants are selected so as to create a diverse community representing a variety of disciplines, experiences, and needs. Selection criteria include the participant's commitment to quality teaching, level of interest in the program, need, openness to new ideas, and potential for contribution to the program as a whole.

With respect to peer consulting, what specific teaching and learning questions and issues do junior faculty bring to this learning community? Applicants to the program are asked to list two or three pressing needs regarding teaching. The 1998–99 list included such issues as keeping students engaged, evaluating students with diverse backgrounds, making large lectures more interactive, using case studies, assessing written and oral communication skills, and getting students to take more responsibility for their own learning.

How can peer consultation effectively address such a wide range of issues? First, I have an opening-closing all-day retreat right after the end of classes in May, at which the "graduating" group meets with the incoming group to "pass the torch." Introductions are followed by a session on teaching problems and solutions, in which small groups of old and new members discuss the teaching needs identified on the applications. This sort of peer consulting works well because the graduating group has developed a very good understanding and expertise about teaching and learning by the end of their year. Throughout the retreat the graduating group shares resources and advice and at the end of the day the new group selects the seminar topics for the first semester of the next year, based on the needs and interests group members have defined.

Second, I take into account that the community members' needs and interests can change greatly each year. Thus we select activities, seminar topics, and leaders by community consensus. During the year, two-hour evening seminars are reserved for topics of broad group interest, such as student intellectual development. One-hour luncheon seminars cover issues of narrower interest, such as interactive media. Over the course of the year the members move from wanting an expert to lead a seminar to offering to lead the seminars themselves. Community begins to build early in the year, especially during an overnight retreat. The safe community that develops allows the members and director to share wisdom and concerns quite freely.

Third, junior faculty community members establish relationships with their experienced faculty mentors (Cox, 1997). Each junior faculty member selects one or two mentors based on perceived need and interests. At the opening/closing retreat the new group receives a list of all continuing faculty members who have served as mentors in the past, along with the names of their protégés. They also receive Miami's *faculty teaching resource list,* which indicates by teaching and learning topic (112 topics for 1998–99) the 175 or so faculty who have volunteered to share their experiences related to these topics. During the year the mentors become peer consultants for their protégés. Student consultants also can play a helpful role, although difficulties sometimes arise because the junior faculty are often inexperienced in working with students in this type of endeavor (Cox and Sorenson, in press).

Peer consulting is an important aspect of another program objective: nurturing the scholarship of teaching. The junior faculty members are gradually introduced to the teaching and learning literature as the seminars and their teaching projects unfold. In November they attend Miami's Lilly Conference on College Teaching and are able to meet some of the teaching scholars whose works they have been reading. In February each member presents a session at a campuswide teaching effectiveness retreat; their topics may be outcomes of the teaching projects or other interests they have developed while in the program. About one-third of the members collaborate and present jointly. After receiving feedback from the retreat, in March they present their work at a national teaching conference. This sequence of events is accompanied by peer consultation with the faculty mentor, with participants in their presentation sessions, with their student consultants, and with other members of the group. In this way these junior faculty develop into teacher-scholars. About 10 percent eventually publish their work in disciplinary or multidisciplinary teaching journals.

Details about the senior faculty learning community, now in its eighth year, are provided by Cox (1998) and Cox and Blaisdell (1995). Community activities and consultation are similar to those in the junior faculty community, although the consultation needs are more mature and complex and include such issues as finding a means for testing the effectiveness of *writing to learn,* developing a new process to train clinician scholars, discovering better ways to grade undergraduate research to motivate continued learning, and examining ideas from nonscientists that might enhance science teaching.

Issue-Focused Faculty Learning Communities. Miami University Faculty Group Using Difference to Enhance Teaching and Learning (Cox, 1998) is an example of an issue-focused faculty learning community. Now in its second year, this group provides an opportunity for eight faculty to participate in a yearlong investigation, dialogue, planning, and implementation of ways to use difference to enhance teaching and learning. The program provides support, both financial and collegial, for implementation of innovative teaching and assessment of outcomes. Each participant has available up to $1,500 to support the investigation and introduction of teaching practices and curricula that address difference and diversity.

The peer consulting in this community proceeds as in the cohort-focused communities, through interactions at an opening-closing retreat in

May, in biweekly seminars throughout the following year, and as a result of attendance at national conferences on diversity. Because of the strong opinions and delicate issues involved, this group works carefully and respectfully to build a safe community.

Outcomes and Effectiveness

Evidence about the success of peer consulting in faculty learning communities comes from two sources. First are the results of annual reports and evaluations that members of the communities complete each year, and second is information from the university-wide seminars that members of each community present in the second semester of the program year.

Annual Reports and Evaluations. We have used the same general report and evaluation form developed over the years since the various programs began: eighteen years in the case of the junior faculty communities, eight years for the senior faculty program, and two years for the community that focuses on difference and diversity. The evaluation deals with impacts of program components on participants and on certain specific outcomes.

Of the eight program components in the junior faculty community, the greatest impact over the past eighteen years has been from learning from the other members of the program, followed by the retreats and conferences, release time, the individual teaching projects, the mentor relationship, seminars, observation of the mentor's or other teachers' classes, and student consultants. The senior faculty and difference and diversity community participants also gave collegiality and learning from other members of the program among the highest impact rating out of several components. The key finding here for the value of peer consultation is that learning from colleagues is seen as the most valuable part of the experience of taking part in a faculty learning community, and this is true regardless of seniority or the issues of main interest.

University-Wide Presentations. More evidence about the positive impact of peer consulting in faculty learning communities is found in what these groups present in their university-wide sessions. The junior faculty community has shared its group and individual learning with others at Miami and beyond. In 1998 the title of their campus and national group presentation was "The Effects of Isolation on Faculty." Other individual or collaborative session topics also reflect the outcomes of their successful consultations and teaching projects. For example, in 1999 these sessions included presentations on interactive learning in large lectures, using simulations, investigating team accomplishment across disciplines, use of journals for teaching and reflection, and using cooperative learning in interdisciplinary groups.

The learning community on difference and diversity has made local and national presentations on using difference to enhance teaching and learning (Cohen, and others, 1999). There is also a teaching portfolio community of faculty, and members of this group share their development each year through presentations that include a display of the portfolios they have developed (see Cox, 1996).

All of these learning communities have had a long-term impact on the university and have helped to build a campuswide teaching and learning culture. For example, Miami teachers who participate in the junior faculty learning community are tenured at a significantly higher rate than those who do not (Cox, 1995), 25 percent of those who serve as senior faculty mentors are graduates of the program (Cox, 1997), and of the 175 faculty who volunteered to be on the 1998–99 faculty teaching resource list, 116 (66 percent) are current or former members of the four learning communities. In 1994, the junior faculty learning community received the Hesburgh Award as the best U.S. faculty development program for enhancing undergraduate teaching. And finally, over the last fifteen years the provost has tripled funding to establish and continue faculty learning communities.

Combining One-on-One and Peer Consultation

The ideal instructional and faculty development program will include both traditional one-on-one and peer consultation in faculty learning communities. When an instructor wants advice both these avenues should be open. If there is a concern about confidentiality or a need for remedial assistance, then one-on-one consultation offered by a professional developer is usually better. And personal advice from a developer may be a more efficient way of dealing with minor items or concerns with narrow focus. But if the need is complex and developmental, then the learning community approach may be better.

For example, someone wanting to put a course syllabus on the World Wide Web in a department that does this routinely may readily get advice without seeking broader interaction with a learning community. But if the teacher is the first in the department to use educational technology, it may be better to join an issue-focused faculty learning community on technology and learning. The community can provide the support, diversity, and expertise of co-adventurers. Other important factors that determine the type of consultation to select are personality type, career stage, and learning style.

In any one year a relatively small number of faculty at an institution may be involved in peer consultation through faculty learning communities, at least compared to the number of faculty using one-on-one consulting services. Yet their enthusiasm and commitment results in the follow-up consulting that they do. This ripple effect makes up for the initially smaller numbers.

Advice on Implementing Faculty Learning Communities

Recommendations for initiating and continuing faculty learning communities can be found in Cox (1995, 1996, 1997). I recommend the following practices for ensuring that such communities include an effective peer consulting component, though it is important to bear in mind that an institution's culture and key players will affect the way in which these suggestions can be most effective.

Initiation. The campus teaching center or faculty development office should plan one faculty learning community at a time; the type of initial cohort-focused or issue-focused community should be determined by a needs analysis. Administrators are often willing to invest funds in junior faculty and in educational technology, so these may be good starting points. Faculty and administrators must be convinced that learning communities will be effective in improving teaching. Evidence from Miami suggests the benefits for faculty are the same as those for student learning communities: increased collaboration across disciplines, better faculty retention, more active learning, and over time, a campus community built around teaching and learning.

Application and Selection. The application for membership in a community must include a section asking about the individual's specific teaching needs, because these needs will form the basis for early group consultation activities. Community members should be selected so as to create a balance across disciplines, interests, experiences, and needs; this will ensure a group of peer consultants with broad and diverse backgrounds.

Prestige. The community can be advertised as an opportunity for faculty to engage in consultation through conversation, a place for scholarly exploration, innovation, and change. Membership should be an honor. The community should not be viewed as a place for remedial consultation for inept or demoralized faculty.

Trust. Peer consultation may involve sharing concerns and frailties with the other members of the learning community. Hence the elements of trust and safety in the community are very important. At the first meeting (and in application information), it is essential to make clear that all discussions are confidential and conducted with respect and openness.

Legacy. For a program in its second or later years, it is a good idea to provide an opportunity for the new members to meet with the graduating members to share various aspects of the program—for example, what they learned, changes they made in their teaching, improvements in student learning, and so forth. The closeness and spirit of those in the graduating community sets a positive tone for peer consulting in the new group.

Activities. The new group should select its own seminar topics, projects, and activities to meet members' needs. An opening seminar topic should be one that interests the new group and has been well received in past years. Collaborative efforts should be encouraged, especially those that give pairs or small groups the chance to undertake and present joint projects and seminars.

Scholarship. Scholarly peer consulting can be nourished by incorporating a sequence of developmental events. For example, the year might start with a discussion based on a book or readings. Later the group can progress to developing teaching projects with clearly stated learning objectives, literature reviews, and assessment plans for student learning.

Assessment. It is important to provide a means for assessing the effectiveness of the peer consulting component of the community, both short- and long-term. A midyear and final evaluation and report in addition to evaluations of each seminar provide evidence of success and ways to improve various aspects of the consulting and the community.

Sharing. Near the end of the year there should be an occasion for peer consultants to share their work with the campus, for example by presenting a university-wide seminar or by circulating a list of members willing to consult with others on specified areas of teaching and learning.

Leadership. The director or coordinator of a faculty learning community should be a well-respected teacher-scholar, be well acquainted with the literature on teaching and learning in higher education, have good consulting abilities, and be a community builder. One of the leaders of a departmental community in the teaching portfolio project at Miami says it well: "Stay flexible! Nothing happens as fast you think it will. Be willing to pause, take valuable side trips dictated by the ebb and flow of the group. Don't push too hard, and listen a lot more than you talk. Good things will happen, but it takes time and will not follow the road map drawn on day one. Also, be sure everyone is having fun and enjoying the process. Eat well. Build a culture of trust and mutual respect. Learn from the diversity and creativity of the individuals in the group."

Challenge. Initiating and maintaining faculty learning communities is fraught with the challenges faced when moving from the teaching paradigm to the learning paradigm. However, the long-term rewards of community and collaboration are well worth it.

In Miami University's faculty teaching development program (Cox, 1998), there are many supports to enable faculty to improve teaching and learning: summer fellowships, teaching leaves, campuswide seminars, grants for teaching evaluation and curriculum development, visiting teacher-scholar programs, learning technology initiatives, small group instructional diagnosis, opportunities for individual consultation, travel funds. But I believe the faculty learning communities and their inherent opportunities for peer consultation continue to have the greatest impact on individuals and the institution.

References

Austin, A. E. "Supporting Junior Faculty Through a Teaching Fellows Program." In M. D. Sorcinelli and A. E. Austin (eds.), *Developing New and Junior Faculty.* New Directions for Teaching and Learning, no. 50. San Francisco: Jossey-Bass, 1992.

Boice, R. *The New Faculty Member: Supporting and Fostering Professional Development.* San Francisco: Jossey-Bass, 1992.

Cohen, M., Cox, M. D., Greeson, L., Jackson, W. S., Kelly, J., and Stevens, M. "Diversity or Difference? Perspectives on and Outcomes of Being a Member of the Faculty

Group Using Difference to Enhance Teaching and Learning." Paper presented at the 11th annual Lilly Conference on College Teaching-West, Lake Arrowhead, Calif., Mar. 5, 1999.

Cox, M. D. "Reclaiming Teaching Excellence: Miami University's Teaching Scholars Program." *To Improve the Academy,* 1994, *13,* 79–96.

Cox, M. D. "The Development of New and Junior Faculty." In W. A. Wright and Associates (eds.), *Teaching Improvement Practices: Successful Strategies for Higher Education.* Bolton, Mass.: Anker, 1995.

Cox, M. D. "A Department-Based Approach to Developing Teaching Portfolios: Perspectives for Faculty Developers." *To Improve the Academy,* 1996, *15,* 275–302.

Cox, M. D. "Long-Term Patterns in a Mentoring Program for Junior Faculty: Recommendations for Practice." *To Improve the Academy,* 1997, *16,* 225–268.

Cox, M. D. *Teaching Grants, Programs, Resources, and Events, 1998–99.* Oxford, Ohio: Miami University, 1998.

Cox, M. D., and Blaisdell, M. "Teaching Development for Senior Faculty: Searching for Fresh Solutions in a Salty Sea." Paper presented at the 20th annual conference of the Professional and Organizational Development Network in Higher Education, North Falmouth, Mass., Oct. 26, 1995.

Cox, M. D., and Sorenson, D. L. "Student Collaboration in Faculty Development." *To Improve the Academy,* in press.

Dewey, J. *How We Think.* Lexington, Mass.: Heath, 1933.

Gabelnick, F., MacGregor, J., Matthews, R. S., and Smith, B. L. (eds.). *Learning Communities: Creating Connections Among Students, Faculty, and Disciplines.* New Directions for Teaching and Learning, no. 41. San Francisco: Jossey-Bass, 1990.

Meiklejohn, A. *The Experimental College.* New York: HarperCollins, 1932.

Sorcinelli, M. D. "New and Junior Faculty Stress: Research and Responses." In M. D. Sorcinelli and A. E. Austin (eds.), *Developing New and Junior Faculty.* New Directions for Teaching and Learning, no. 50. San Francisco: Jossey-Bass, 1992.

Taylor, P. G. "Creating Environments Which Nurture Development: Messages from Research into Academics' Experiences." *International Journal for Academic Development,* 1997, *2,* 42–49.

Tiberius, R. G. "From Shaping Performances to Dynamic Interaction: The Quiet Revolution in Teaching Improvement Programs." In W. A. Wright and Associates, *Teaching Improvement Practices: Successful Strategies for Higher Education.* Bolton, Mass.: Anker, 1995.

Wright, W. A., and O'Neil, M. C. "Teaching Improvement Practices: International Perspectives." In W. A. Wright and Associates, *Teaching Improvement Practices: Successful Strategies for Higher Education.* Bolton, Mass.: Anker, 1995.

MILTON D. COX is university director for teaching effectiveness programs at Miami University, Ohio, founder of the Lilly Conferences on College Teaching, and editor-in-chief of the Journal on Excellence in College Teaching.

6

Action learning is a peer-based approach to teaching consultation, and a potentially powerful method of promoting change and improvement.

Consultation Through Action Learning

Liz Beaty

Improving teaching involves the professional development of the teacher. Even very simple changes to practice, such as using a new computer package to produce overhead projector transparencies, or introducing a different method of group work into seminars, requires a teacher to develop new skills and apply them appropriately in a particular course. Teachers must think not only about student learning but also about their own ability to use techniques and methods skillfully. Starting to improve an aspect of teaching means acquiring knowledge and skills; this turns the teacher into a learner, and improving teaching becomes a professional development project.

Action learning is a continuous process of learning and reflection, supported by colleagues, with an intention of getting things done (McGill and Beaty, 1995). Individuals work on real problems and learn from reflection on their practice over time. The process "helps people to take an active stance toward life and helps to overcome the tendency to be passive toward the pressures of life and work" (p. 11). It involves regular meetings in groups known as *sets,* where the focus is on the issues and problems that individuals bring. Each person plans future action with the structured attention and support of the group. It is a process that supports learning from experience.

Action learning has been used extensively since the 1970s for management development and has spread to other professional areas (Pedlar, 1992). More recently action learning has found its way into higher education, initially through use in graduate courses (Bourner, Frost, and Beaty, 1992) and later as a process to support courses for higher education teachers (Beaty, 1997). Because of its focus on learning from experience, action learning is particularly appropriate for supporting consultation to improve teaching. It includes a strong element of peer consultation alongside facilitation provided by experienced educational development specialists. This chapter describes how action learning can be used to support consultation, using a case study example that illustrates its use in a British university.

Improving Teaching Through Reflective Practice

In order to improve, a teacher needs to learn from experience over time. Experience does not of itself improve practice. Rather, thoughtful and critical reflection on previous practice invokes the necessary learning and change. This process has been captured in various descriptions of an experiential learning cycle, as outlined by Kolb (1984). In Kolb's cycle reflecting on experience allows for generalization of principles that might apply to other situations, which in turn facilitates the process of planning for change. Implementing such change leads to new experiences, further reflection and generalization, and so on.

In making a deliberate attempt to learn experientially, learners build on their experience and reflect on what happened, how they felt about it, and how it relates to similar experiences. Starting from these reflections, the learner is able to generalize about the type of experience it was, using relevant ideas and concepts to make sense of the experience. The learner then thinks about what might improve the situation or what might be done in a similar future situation, and makes plans to test this out in practice. This *experiment* produces new experience with which to continue the cycle.

The cycle demonstrates that reflection alone is not sufficient for development to occur. To learn from experience the teacher needs to ask, "So what? What is signified by this experience that could inform my future practice?" Planning for change then follows naturally from systematic reflection on practice.

Action informed by experiential learning is a useful key to professional development. Development is, however, rarely simple. Just recognizing that improvement is necessary, even identifying how this could be achieved, is not enough. Improvement often requires the teacher to make a difference in professional practice through acquiring new knowledge or skills.

Improvements may depend on changes to the learning environment rather than personal change by the teacher. Some changes can be made by an individual decision, but others require discussion with colleagues and collaborative decisions. Thus change often requires a team approach.

Change is unlikely to be right the first time and therefore will require further evaluation and modifications. Development of teaching is cyclical, needing a structured process of evaluation and change in both professional practice and the broader learning environment.

Supporting Reflective Practice Through Dialogue

Even on projects that are largely within the control of an individual teacher, reflecting, conceptualizing, and planning can be considerably enhanced by consultation with others. The support of peers provides an opportunity for learning beyond individual reflection. An important way to improve teaching is therefore to find ways to focus dialogue with others on areas that need development.

The teacher can generally rely on peers to empathize and can trust their professional ability to maintain confidentiality. Experienced colleagues can use their knowledge and insight to illuminate reflections on practice. Unlike students, peers notice the teacher's actions from the point of view of a professional. They are also able to imagine reactions to suggested changes for the future. A colleague's knowledge of the discipline can be an important focus for this reflection. A peer who is not in the same subject area can give the teacher feedback on the methods used if not the course content. Consulting with colleagues also emphasizes teaching as a team activity. Students rely on many instructors for their learning, and hence it is more effective for teachers to work together with colleagues to facilitate that learning.

Although discussions support reflective practice, a general conversation rarely probes a teacher's own particular experience in any specific or deep way. It is easy for a group of teachers to discuss teaching and learning, for example, without drawing any conclusions about their own teaching. The concentrated and intentional process of reflecting in order to improve teaching with the aid of peers requires a more structured process. Action learning provides a potent tool for improving teaching through peer consultation.

How Action Learning Works

Action learning is based on the idea that effective learning and development have to be about real problems in real life with real people. As a support for learning through dialogue, this process is distinctive because of the importance placed on understanding a situation in order to take action.

The key components of action learning are as follows:

Individuals meet together in a set. For ease of working, about five to seven people make up the set.

Each individual brings a real issue or project to the set that they wish to work on.

Learning comes from the experience of undertaking the project; it is important that teachers identify projects in which they have authority to take action (individually or collaboratively).

Action learning sets have a set adviser to facilitate the process of learning from experience, to monitor the structure of reflection and action planning, and to review progress over time.

Regular set meetings are held: for example three-hour meetings every four weeks over an agreed period of six months or a year.

During the set, members negotiate explicit ground rules to ensure effective working.

At the set meeting, time is shared evenly among the participants so that each takes time to reflect on progress and to agree on action plans. This reflection is aided by appropriate support and challenge from the other set members.

The aim is for all participants to learn from reflection on their experience and be able to make progress with their projects by planning the next steps.

The action learning sets support the learning cycle so that results are seen in relation to both the project and the professional development of participants.

Action Learning Projects

The choice of project for action learning can be broad. It would be inefficient to use this approach when there is an obvious straightforward answer to a problem: in these cases, it is better to use an expert who can guide the particular development needed. But many problems in teaching are not easily answered by reading or seeking guidance from an expert, and action learning can be especially helpful with these more intangible issues.

Most problems have an inner and an outer domain: the inner feelings and thoughts about an event and the outer world of the environment in which it occurs. In the action learning set, individuals can learn through reflection on their progress, and in doing so they learn about themselves as well as about the project they are undertaking. Take for example a teacher who wants to develop her ability to supervise student teamwork. The project starts out by focusing on methods of supervision, techniques for getting students to work effectively in teams, and so on. Through reflecting on her own supervisory interactions, the teacher may recognize that some of her interventions seem to help the students' progress but other actions do not. She may also notice that she works more effectively with groups that have a natural leader: does this mean that her attention is focused unevenly on the group? Here her reflections take her deeper into the realm of interpersonal skills and issues of interaction. She discovers that the project, which started out objective and clear, has become more subjective and more personal.

However a project may be defined initially, improving teaching is likely to move between objective and subjective issues. Dealing with teaching projects usually involves this mix of the objective and the subjective, of technique and interpersonal skill. Thus supporting the development of teaching crucially involves supporting the development of the teacher. Action learning provides this support to the individual while focusing energy on his or her ability to act. Like all consultation methods, action learning is contextualized. Exploring the issues and reasons for progress or identifying blocks to change leads to action planning; the aim is to find room to maneuver in the situation or to identify the next step in developing personal knowledge and skill.

Because action learning is a group method, participants also learn a great deal by listening as other participants discuss work on their projects. As they hear other set members explore their issues, thoughts are directed to similarities and differences in teaching approaches. Thus some of the insights that occur in action learning sets are serendipitous. The spirit of being "comrades in diversity" (Revans, 1983), of sharing a mission and a culture of reflection, creates a supportive background for taking risks through innovation. It also motivates through the commitment to regular attendance at the set meetings. Frequently after the original time agreement has ended, sets of individuals who find the process both stimulating and supportive will continue or form new sets.

The Role of the Adviser

Action learning sets, however, are not simply self-help groups. Taking real projects and allocating time for each person to work on exploring issues gives a structured focus to the intention to evaluate and change. It is important that this opportunity for peer consultation does not degenerate into a griping session or a collusive blaming of others. Nor should action learning sets offer expert counseling. Although certain counseling skills, especially listening and empathy, are useful for exploring projects in the set, the focus should be on planning for action. The intention is not to explore the psychological health of the individual, nor to go deeply into past experience. Inevitably, exploring issues of professional practice does bring to conscious attention behavior patterns that can block progress. But the business of the set is usually best accomplished by focusing on the project and suggesting that psychological issues be followed up if necessary with a trained counselor.

Action learning sets are usually facilitated by an experienced set adviser. The role of the adviser is to support the process of learning. On the practical side, facilitation ensures that all set members have equal time to explore their projects and that action points are recorded. These functions can, however, be shared among the group. Supporting the process is a complex task that requires having empathy with individual set members as they present issues and careful monitoring of the type of intervention that is helpful to the progress of the project and the learning that comes from reflection.

At different times and in relation to different aspects of their projects, teachers will be more or less vulnerable. It is the job of the set adviser to make sure that when teachers present their projects, they are offered appropriate support and challenge in order to promote development and learning. The set adviser will encourage all members of the set to use open, exploratory questions and to leave silence for the presenter to think through issues. The set members will be encouraged to seek action plans that come from the teacher's own analysis of the situation rather than to give advice from their own perspective. In time, facilitation becomes part of every set member's role as participants become accustomed to the skills required. Even people who are very skilled in group dynamics have found it useful to have a facilitator in an action learning set to take the pressure off participants and allow them to concentrate fully on their own issues.

In action learning, individuals are seen as being experts on their own projects. This model of consultation aims to help teachers develop their teaching by helping them learn from their experience. This contrasts with consultation, which is about transferring expertise. There is of course room in set meetings for passing on the experience of others, and this can come from identifying the need during discussions and making an action plan that includes gaining such knowledge. The time spent in the set meetings simply makes learning and development much more focused and efficient.

Action Learning in Action: Developing Teaching Portfolios

The Dearing Report, the recent British government commission report on higher education, called for greater professionalism in teaching practice. One result of this has been further development of a professional qualification for teachers (Staff and Educational Development Association, 1992; National Committee of Inquiry into Higher Education, 1997). In April 1999, a new organization, the Institute for Learning and Teaching, began accrediting programs of professional development for teachers in the United Kingdom, with membership in the institute contingent on completion of such a program. It is likely that membership in the institute will also be offered to experienced academic staff who can present a portfolio that documents evidence of the teacher's professional practice.

Coventry University has had a postgraduate course for teachers in higher education since the early 1990s; a program based on this course has recently been designed to allow experienced staff to gain the qualification through accreditation of prior learning. This program is based on action learning and the development of an individual teaching portfolio to meet the standard for accreditation.

Participants in the program are all experienced members of staff with over five years' teaching experience. They are grouped into action learning sets of up to seven members, and each set has an adviser who is an experienced educational development consultant. The set adviser also takes the role of tutor, offering tutorials, observation of teaching, and formative assessment of the portfolio as it develops.

The program lasts a year and includes two half-day workshops to introduce the theory of reflective practice and action learning that underpins the program and to brief participants on the requirements for teaching observation. Action learning sets then meet for three hours each month. After a meeting the set adviser records action points for each member of the set.

Between meetings the participants record their reflections on teaching events and gather evidence from practice for their portfolio.

The basic project is the same for all members: the development of their teaching and the building of a teaching portfolio. However, the nature of the portfolio differs according to the particular teaching role, discipline, and teaching style of the participant. At set meetings individuals take turns to present progress on portfolio development. This involves bringing portfolio entries for discussion. The set members help each presenter to explore the rationale for their teaching approach based on the evidence in the portfolio.

The teachers learn a great deal from this exploration. Reflections cover ethical issues as well as difficulties with particular methods or groups of students. Experiences in different subject areas are compared, and ideas and practical solutions are transferred from one subject area to another. Although direct advice is not given as part of the set process, it is frequently offered and followed up separately. The set adviser and members bring relevant resources to help with the particular teaching issues that arise during these meetings. These might include examples of teaching material, papers on theories of learning, or hints and tips on using particular teaching methods.

At points throughout the program, observation of teaching practice is required. This is undertaken in the spirit of developing reflective practice and not as an appraisal tool. The feedback is formative and constructive, with the aim of improving areas of practice identified by the teacher. The observer (or consultant) can be a member of the set, the set adviser, or another colleague. Choice of observer will depend on the participant's issue or learning focus. If the purpose is to reflect on the progress of a class, then it might be best to ask the educational developer to observe. But if the main interest is in, say, whether teaching is at the right level for a particular group of students, a colleague experienced in the discipline might be more appropriate. In any event, exploring the feedback from the observer can become a focus of the set meeting. The observer's comments with the teacher's reflections and follow-up actions become part of the teaching portfolio.

Thus consultation becomes an organic part of the process and is often the subject of action points decided in the set meeting. A typical set of action points for one participant following a set meeting might be:

George's Action Points, November 20, 1998
- Talk to Jane about her use of self-assessment in group work.
- Read the chapter on students working in teams suggested by Tom.
- Try out Liz's idea on structuring group work with second-year students on Tuesday next week.
- Get feedback from students using the quick questionnaire in Smith's book.
- Arrange for Jenny to observe the session and give me feedback.
- Write up reflections after getting feedback from Jenny.
- Put the session outline, feedback, and reflections in my portfolio.

These action points illustrate the rich environment for consultation created by the action learning process. The intention is to learn through reflective practice, and due to the shared experience of action learning these reflections are enriched through consultation offered as the project is explored. The final portfolio is assessed by the teacher, who checks the contents against the requirements for accreditation. Peer assessment in the set ensures that the portfolio covers all the necessary areas to an appropriate standard. The final assessment is undertaken by the set adviser and checked by a second member of the course team. The portfolio is then submitted for validation through the normal assessment committee procedures.

Conclusion

Consultation to improve teaching requires an emphasis on reflection, informed evaluation, and action planning. Colleagues can support this process by being involved in constructive peer consultation. Action learning offers a structured group process to support peer learning from experience. The experience in Britain, outlined in this chapter, supports the idea that using action learning as a consultation method is a valuable way to ensure that professional development and improvement in teaching are successfully fused.

References

Beaty, L. "Developing Reflective Practice." In *SEDA Induction Pack*. London: Staff and Educational Development Association, 1997.

Bourner, T., Frost, P., and Beaty, L. "Management Development by Research." *Personnel Review,* 1992, 21 (2).

Kolb, D. *Experiential Learning: Experience as the Source of Learning and Development.* Upper Saddle River, N.J.: Prentice Hall, 1984.

McGill, I., and Beaty, L. *Action Learning: A Guide for Professional, Management and Educational Development.* (2nd ed.) London: Kogan Page, 1995.

National Committee of Inquiry into Higher Education. *Higher Education in the Learning Society.* The Dearing Report. London: National Committee of Inquiry into Higher Education, 1997.

Pedlar, M. (ed.). *Action Learning in Practice.* (2nd ed.) Aldershot, England: Gower, 1992.

Revans, R. "Action Learning: Its Origins and Nature." In M. Pedlar (ed.), *Action Learning in Practice.* Aldershot, England: Gower, 1983.

Staff and Educational Development Association. *Scheme for the Accreditation of Teachers in Higher Education.* Birmingham, England: Staff and Educational Development Association, 1992.

LIZ BEATY is head of Learning Development at Coventry University, England, and a former vice chair of the Staff and Educational Development Association in the United Kingdom.

7

How can we get faculty to use constructive criticism to improve teaching just as we do to improve research?

Consultation Using Critical Friends

Gunnar Handal

Criticism has always enjoyed a strong position in the academic world, both in rhetoric and practice. A common element of scientific work is a critical approach to accepted interpretations and explanations. Without criticism of existing knowledge we would experience almost no scientific progress. Thus criticizing other researchers' reports and publications is an accepted activity. It is carried out by means of comprehensive refereeing procedures in the case of scientific and professional publications and conferences. Another ritualized example is the thesis defense, a key element in the evaluation and approval of graduate degrees. This is how the critical tradition is passed on in academia. New members of the academy are socialized into this central aspect of academic culture by acting as spectators or personally taking part in a rite of passage.

At times such criticism can be merciless—particularly between competing or antagonistic groups or between different schools of researchers. More often, however, it is not. Good criticism is generally relevant, argumentative, well documented, and instructive. There are many times when criticism is very positive.

This is why some scholars prefer the French term *critique*. This connotes the type of criticism that takes place in the arts, where a connoisseur in the field comments on the positive and negative aspects of an artistic work (a painting, book, play, film), based on his or her professional judgment and usually in a public forum. Learning to live in an academic culture entails, among other things, tackling the roles of giving and taking criticism in ways that are accepted by this culture. To a varying degree, we are all masters of this genre, and those who are really proficient receive high esteem.

NEW DIRECTIONS FOR TEACHING AND LEARNING, no. 79, Fall 1999 © Jossey-Bass Publishers

We might say that this is one of the skills that scholars within the university system must develop to gain recognition as competent members of the academic profession. Practicing criticism professionally can be done in various ways, but there are clear (albeit local) limits for acceptable forms, limits that must not be transgressed if you wish to retain the profession's respect and loyalty. Further, the content of the criticism put forward must be rooted in the accepted and valid norms within the culture (the department, discipline, or research community).

Criticism of Research—and of Teaching

Why do I write so much about research in a book about university teaching? Because I believe that we lack corresponding traditions in academic culture when it comes to teaching. Educators engage relatively rarely in systematic appraisal of their colleagues' teaching in the form of a critical evaluation that is carried out publicly, as in the case of scholarly criticism. In keeping with the reigning culture, it is not wholly acceptable. University-level teaching is more or less the private property of the individual instructor, and any commentary could be construed as meddling.

Among the questions we posed in an interview survey carried out among the participants in a faculty development course some years ago was this one: "Do you often talk with colleagues about their teaching?" One of the participants answered in horror, "No, that would be comparable to speaking to them about their personal hygiene."

Of course I know that this is not a universal response. Some university lecturers do communicate with their peers about one another's teaching. I also assume that the situation in colleges and universities in other countries could differ from that in my own (Norway). Still, I contend that the description is reasonably valid for much of university culture worldwide.

In many parts of the world the past decade has seen increasing public criticism of the quality of teaching and learning in higher education. Student evaluations of teaching, common for many years in North America, have found their way to Europe and Australia. Here it is the "users" of higher education who are offering the criticism, rather than colleagues. And in some cases the evidence from these evaluations is rejected on the grounds that the criticism is essentially unprofessional.

Other more comprehensive assessments of university teaching and curricula have been undertaken at a program- or institution-wide level, often initiated and controlled by government agencies (Jordell, 1992). Although these evaluations are often made by academics serving on assessment bodies, these individuals may have been conscripted to do so and are not primarily offering criticism on behalf of the academy. In some countries (such as the Netherlands), universities have taken on the task of carrying out nationwide evaluations of entire disciplines, but this happened mainly to prevent the Ministry of Education from doing the task itself.

Why So Little Criticism of Teaching?

Assuming it is true that the academic culture is often reluctant to practice internal, collegial criticism of teaching at universities, what are the reasons? Let me offer a few.

Teaching doesn't really matter. Do we perceive teaching as such a secondary concern for the university and for ourselves as educators that we don't consider collegial and critical scrutiny worth the effort? Hardly. In more than two decades of work in faculty development, I have found that many university educators care deeply about their teaching. They deem it important and put a lot of work into it.

University lecturers are already outstanding professional educators. Consequently it would be superfluous for their teaching to be submitted to anything but self-criticism (and perhaps occasional feedback from students). I do not think that this is a common belief among university faculty. In any case it lacks validity when we consider how systematically research is subjected to peer review.

Getting university educators to change their teaching methods is a hopeless task. The argument here is that faculty feel so constrained by the academic environment that they simply teach as they think best, and there is little motivation for change. Criticism from peers is therefore unwelcome. Many university teachers probably subscribe in part to this view, but empirically it proves unsatisfactory. There are too many examples of educators and institutions that do change their curricula and teaching methods because of internal criticism of existing practice.

University educators are not professional teachers. They are therefore not equipped to offer informed criticism and to respond to such criticism. Let me stress that this is not to discredit the erudition and expertise of university teachers. They are certainly professionals in their disciplinary fields. However, the *teaching* of a subject is a different type of activity, which in principle demands its own type of professionalism. Is it unfair to expect university educators to be doubly professional?

What It Means to Be a Professional Educator

Belonging to a profession entails (1) a lengthy higher education in your field, (2) a comprehensive shared and scientifically based knowledge base for carrying out your work, and (3) a shared professional code of ethics.

University educators in their roles as researchers or scientists and scholars meet these demands, but not in their roles as *teachers* of their subjects. Though teaching is a major part of an academic's job, many faculty members lack awareness of their professional responsibilities as teachers.

In keeping with our conception of ourselves as professionals and researchers in our chosen fields, we subordinate ourselves to an array of scientific quality demands and norms. These demands relate to our methods of inquiry, the way we write scientific articles, and our research ethics. We subordinate ourselves to these demands because it seems reasonable and because it is a prerequisite to achieving recognition, acceptance, and even protection from the professional group. Indeed, the norms of the profession were created by its members to ensure the quality of their own work and to protect their own interests. This is one of the instruments for achieving society's acceptance of the profession's autonomy. The norms can be altered by initiatives within the profession, but they require conformity as long as they last and are enforced through active sanctions.

When it comes to teaching, most of us accept having little influence on the time and place where our assigned duties are carried out. We might grumble, but we accept these. I believe it is harder for us to accept demands to teach in a particular way to meet common norms for good teaching. Such norms have not been created within the bounds of our profession, partly because they are regarded as involving a sphere of activity that is private.

Let me cite an example. In Norway we have rules of research ethics that are shared by large groups of researchers (NESH, 1994), but we have no common ethical code for teaching. The only example of such a code I have found is in Canada, where guidelines were developed by the Society for Teaching and Learning in Higher Education (Murray and others, 1996). We recently developed ethical guidelines for research supervision (UiO, 1997) at my own university, and this provoked some strong reactions among the faculty.

I do not necessarily consider existing written guidelines on the ethics of teaching or supervision to be ideal, but the negative reaction among the university teachers illustrates our uncertainty about our professionalism as teachers (Handal, 1997). It may be unrealistic to expect all academics to develop complete dual professionalism in our disciplinary fields as well as in our teaching. But I do think that universities should aim at encouraging enhanced pedagogical professionalism. In this connection, it is vital that the individual university professor is conscious of the categorical divide between *individual freedom* (to do what I want) and *professional autonomy* (acting within the norms of the professional group).

Enhanced professionalism can be achieved through becoming acquainted with concepts, theories, and research on teaching methods and student learning processes. This is a necessary basic investment if faculty members are to cooperate on the development of their teaching and communicate meaningfully with each other. We need a common language that includes concepts with some basis in systematized knowledge and theory about teaching.

There are other prerequisites. The institution should make time and space for informed discourse about teaching, respond to the needs of faculty to learn more about teaching issues, and provide mechanisms to recognize faculty members' competence for the educational part of their job.

This recognition must be minted in the system's own currency: due emphasis in relation to appointment, tenure, and promotion.

Colleagues as Critical Friends

My objective here is to look more specifically into mutual criticism among colleagues and its potential as a strategy for consultation. This ties in with my wish for increased professionalism in university teaching. If the quality of teaching and learning is to improve, it is vital that those who instigate educational development have ownership of the process, that they understand and approve of it. Such changes will demand joint, not just individual, efforts and require communication and collaboration between the involved parties in reaching common understanding and practice.

In the literature about development of educational institutions we come across the concept of the *critical friend* (Simons, 1987; Tiller, 1990). This implies an interesting combination of concepts that we usually do not associate: friendship and criticism. Friends are people who are close to us, who support us, and who provide confirmation. They often disregard our weak points or excuse them rather than confront us with them. Criticism is generally conveyed by others who are not as close to us, perhaps our superiors or representatives of viewpoints different from our own. But in fact a real friend is someone to rely on, someone who will hold a critical mirror before us if necessary.

Let me draw another parallel with research. Consider the following situation. A younger colleague, Stephen, approaches you with his nearly completed thesis. His supervisor has made it clear that the work should soon be ready to submit. But both Stephen and his supervisor want a second opinion from you. Stephen is a congenial fellow, and you have developed a solid and friendly relationship with him after working together for several years. The funding period for his research grant is now drawing to an end, so it is important that he wind up his thesis work. You read the thesis and have your doubts about its quality. But you see that with some revising, the clarification of a few concepts, and a sharper summary of the results, it would be excellent. In its present form, however, submitting the thesis for evaluation would be risky. Another semester of work is needed to ensure its quality. The two of you have an appointment to discuss the thesis, and with his buoyant spirits and his aura of expectation, Stephen arrives.

Most of us would feel that the responsible thing to do, as his good friend, would be to say, "Stephen, I'm sorry but I think that you still have more work to do on this thesis. Look here . . ." You would be letting him down as a genuine friend if you stifled your criticism and chose a more comfortable approach, "Great, Stephen, you've done a wonderful job. Maybe there are a few things that could be polished up, but I'm sure you will see them yourself when you reread the entire text. Good luck!"

A good critical friendship involves an obligation to analyze and criticize. Your friend has come to you confident both that you will give an honest and well-founded response and that you have the competence and ability to provide it; this is the response he seeks, rather than a nonchalant pat on the shoulder. In other words, a critical friendship includes

- A personal relationship of confidence
- Belief in the professional competence of the critical friend
- Expectation of personal integrity
- Basic trust in the good intentions of the critical friend

Critical Friends and University Teaching

At the institutional level, I think that a department that is concerned about the quality of its teaching could invite an individual or a small group of critical friends to evaluate the program. They would have to be people known and respected for their competence. The mission would be to look at the curriculum and teaching methods used in the department, observe selected key courses, talk with instructors and students, and give a critical response to what they have seen, heard, and thought about. The department or institution might specify particular aspects of the curriculum for attention, but it must be inherent in the "contract" between them that the critical friends can broach other aspects that they deem important.

In this situation we would expect criticism to take place in a context of collegiality. It would be a type of criticism that primarily takes the institution's own intentions as its point of departure and proceeds to offer commentary in that spirit. At the same time the critical friends might be encouraged to reflect critically on these very intentions, to see whether they are appropriate and worthwhile. Perhaps they might also reveal some unintended outcomes of the program, for instance that students might be becoming less independent than intended, due to a heavy workload or highly prescribed curriculum, a side effect that the institution had neither sought nor considered.

I have had the opportunity to function as a critical friend for a teacher education program at a Swedish college (Handal, 1996). It turned out to be a valuable experience for the institution and also most instructive for me. Serving as a critical friend at the institutional level is something that is hard to take on at one's own institution, where the consultant is an integral part of the system and the culture. But visiting another university in this role provides an opportunity for inspiration and generating new ideas precisely because of the different environment that is seen with fresh eyes. As an additional benefit, acting as a critical friend makes the consultant aware of aspects of his or her own practice that have not necessarily been considered before. This is a benefit of critical friendship that should not be underestimated. It can be as gainful for the critical friend as for the institution or people who are receiving the observations and comments.

Perhaps we can recognize something here from comparable experiences in research. When doing peer reviews of articles and conference papers or when reading a thesis and serving as an external examiner, we usually learn a lot ourselves. We get new ideas, become acquainted with fresh research, and are made aware of different perspectives and methods. Moreover, we might discover that our own criticism mirrors criticism that others have directed toward our own work.

A variation of such institutional use of critical friends is the system of *benchmarking*. The department or program engages people from an institution that it wishes to be compared to and requests them to analyze a program or practice. This is a way for an organization to gauge itself against a standard and ferret out possible weak points.

I am convinced from my own experience that the same process of peer review and collegial consultation can be used on the *individual* level. There are advantages to doing so. One is the obvious need for a fresh look at methods the teacher may not know need updating. Here a colleague can offer advice on what can be improved and how to make the changes.

Another advantage, and perhaps a more important one, is that much of our teaching is so dependent upon material and social frameworks (among them the contributions of our colleagues) that the prospects for making any substantial change of practice through individual efforts are limited. John Elliot, a veteran in the work to change the English education system, said a few years ago that "individual teachers cannot significantly improve their practices in isolation without opportunities for discussion with professional peers and others operating in a significant role-relationship to them" (Elliot, 1992, p. 25).

There are several pertinent points in this quotation. First, it is difficult for teachers working on their own to bring about meaningful change. Several colleagues have to be involved. Second, changes require the opportunity for discussions with colleagues. Third, these partners in discourse must be not just colleagues, but professionals. In other words they must have the required competence to analyze, discuss, and critique the teaching concerned. Fourth, people outside the teacher's immediate range of colleagues can be especially useful in such discourse by offering perspectives that are not bound by the limited local context. However, as a prerequisite, the external consultant must have a special relationship to the other educators. He or she must be considered, in the term of Berger and Luckmann (1971), as a *significant other*—a person whose viewpoints are respected, who is listened to, and who can serve as a role model. This is what I mean by the critical friend.

Critical Friendship in Collegial Consultation

We can also learn to function as critical friends for each other in the local context. And if you are invited by a colleague to serve in this way, it is a declaration of confidence in you and your competence and of trust that you will take the task seriously.

Before taking on this role you might want to talk a little more with your colleague about his or her teaching goals so as to get a background for making an interpretation. This requires listening, and although you must be sure that you understand these goals, this is not the time to begin taking a critical look at them.

So now you are ready to observe some teaching. Above all you must bear in mind your colleague's intentions and judge the teaching in this context. If the colleague has expressed a straightforward wish to disseminate information, you have to witness what happens and relate it to the criteria for such teaching. Is the structure of the presentation clear? Is it understandable for the students? Is the presentation adapted to their abilities, previous knowledge, and so on? As Kierkegaard (1859) said, you must "first and foremost find the place where the other is, and start from there. If you cannot do that, then you cannot help him" (my translation).

But you must also look for other aspects of the instruction that your colleague has not talked about. How do the students react to the lecture? Do the lecturer's examples illustrate the issue and function as well for both male and female students? Or would it have been better if the students had been given an opportunity to ask questions, even if this is contrary to the lecturer's intentions?

Afterward you can talk together. What do you answer to your colleague's question, "How do you think it went?" Even if you think so, your immediate response should not be, "You should have allowed for much more student participation." First you have to concentrate on your colleague's proclaimed intentions for the lecture so that he or she receives an answer that relates to these goals. Only when this has been done should you discuss the goals themselves. "What, really, are your teaching goals?" "How do you conceive of student learning?" "Is this the best way to use teaching time?" "How do you want the students to prepare for the next lecture? Are they in fact doing that?"

As a critical friend I do not always have an answer to all the questions or perspectives I raise. But I must have the imagination (and wisdom) to ask them so that we can consider them together (Handal and Lauvås, 1987). Above all, you must take your assignment seriously. You have been invited in to provide serious criticism, in the same way as you would as a critic of a scholarly paper. It would be insufficient to say, "Yes, this was great. Just tell me if you want me to come back another time."

From Occasional to Systematic Consultation

The above example is individual and one-way (one person has invited a colleague to come and observe an occasional lecture). An extension of this idea is the establishment of a collaborative *reflective team* of teachers (Lycke, 1998) who examine one another's teaching as critical friends and discuss the themes, dilemmas, and critical points they observe, with the aim of becoming wiser and better educators together. Obviously these discussions can also include students' perceptions and evaluations, but in this context only as an aid in colleagues' mutual scrutiny of their own teaching.

In these reflective teams, where members act as each other's critical friends, an external critical friend can also be most helpful. The advantage of the outsider is that he or she has a different perspective, is not part and parcel of the same culture, does not always take the same things for granted, and can often rejuvenate the discussion with these outside perspectives and experiences.

To make this clearer, we can borrow some ideas from *hermeneutics*, the science of interpretation; especially applicable to the interpretation of texts, it can also apply to situations. The cardinal idea here is to grasp what the text was supposed to convey, what the author really intended. In addition, a more critical form of hermeneutics is practiced when we try to fathom why the author in fact wrote a text and how it made sense to do so in this way and in the context of the day. Such critical hermeneutics can include aspects, norms, and interpretations that were not known, not relevant, or simply not considered when the text was written; the text can be interpreted from these perspectives.

The reason for touching on hermeneutics is to illustrate that self-interpretation of one's own practice is limited to the perspectives that one already has, whereas the sort of hermeneutics we engage in with colleagues provides much greater potential for helpful criticism. However, benefiting fully from such critical hermeneutics often entails opening our practice up to a critical friend who represents other perspectives, concepts, knowledge, and models than are readily accessible within the culture.

Critical Friendship and Faculty Development

In our faculty development courses at the University of Oslo we include work in what we have called *collegial tutor groups*. Groups of three or four course participants visit each other's teaching sessions. They engage in pre- and postteaching conferences and tutor each other. The roles of mutual critical friends are practiced within the groups. We have found it interesting to observe that when these collegial clusters are heterogeneously assembled with teachers from various fields, the participants usually act more as external critical friends for one another. This is because they represent disparate experiences, view different things as self-evident, and are more likely to ask each other authentic and essential questions, such as, "Why do you do things this way?" As course instructors, we have joined these groups and found that with our special expertise we can also have positions as external critical friends. Again, an essential requirement for success is a relationship of mutual confidence and respect between the critic and colleague. Or, as the Danish writer Piet Hein puts it, there are two requirements: "first to win each other's trust and second, to deserve it."

Mutual Demands on Critical Friends

From my perspective, it is important that those who function in such roles try to develop their knowledge about the issues they are critiquing and that they link experiential insights to concepts and theories that are empirically grounded in relevant educational research. I am not asserting that all university teachers should become professional pedagogues, but in their aspirations toward more professional teaching they should try to acquire some basic knowledge from the educational literature. After all, an art critic lacking a working knowledge of the basic concepts and tenets of aesthetics would have a slim chance of being taken seriously as a critical friend. Teaching is no different.

From this perspective, we make certain demands of critical friends in order to benefit from their advice. Likewise there are demands on those who choose to seek help from a critical friend. Be they institutions or individuals, I believe that they will first need *courage*. A healthy dose of self-confidence is required to invite someone to observe something as personal as teaching. Inviting a critical friend to watch an activity you have not completely mastered is difficult; showing off something you do brilliantly is easier.

The other need is a *willingness to change*. If we are quite certain that our teaching is being carried out just the way we want it, we should not invite a critical friend to observe it. The invitation must originate from the notion that we have something to learn and a wish to change our work to make it better. If this willingness is lacking, every attempt at constructive criticism is likely to devolve into a why-don't-we-yes-but game in which all suggestions are repelled or excused with arguments such as, "We have already done that. It doesn't work here. Our situation is so special that . . ."

The Bottom Line: Freedom and Control

This touches on a central conflict that I mentioned earlier between the views of university teaching as an individual and as a collective phenomenon. I stated that many university teachers perceive their teaching as essentially private property. This can be partially explained by again drawing a parallel with research. Freedom of research is a strong academic ideal. The academic culture is deeply ingrained with the principle of liberty to pursue the hypotheses that the researcher considers important. The ideal of free scholarly inquiry is cherished and protected, despite a world where so much research is steered by the market or fashion and constrained by funding opportunities.

I find that this ideal is rather indiscriminately transferred to academic teaching and transformed into an academic right to assemble any listeners who wish to gather in front of the lectern and to convey whatever knowledge, opinions, and criticisms are thought to be important. Certainly it is important that teachers be free to express their views on issues on which they are experts. But there are other requirements of an effective university teacher. Much teaching involves fulfillment of a social contract to educate new generations of students and serve the broader needs of society. Coherent curricula and quality student learning depend on cooperation and a measure of control. *Control* has a negative connotation, especially in contrast with the idea of academic freedom. But if teaching is to become more professional, it may be that we will have to respect some common norms for good teaching and to collaborate among ourselves as critical friends in a joint attempt to achieve these norms. We have long done so for research, so why not also for teaching?

References

Berger, P. L., and Luckmann, T. *The Social Construction of Reality. A Treatise in the Sociology of Knowledge.* Harmondsworth, England: Penguin Books, 1971.

Elliot, J. "What Have We Learned from Action Research in School-Based Evaluation?" In *Theory and Practice of School-Based Evaluation: A Research Perspective.* Report of the conference held at Oppland College, Lillehammer, Norway, 1992.

Handal, G. *Lærerutdanning ved Högskolan i Örebro. Kommentarer til Deler av Utdanningen fra en "Kritisk Venn"* (Teacher education at the College of Örebro. Comments to part of the program from a "critical friend"). Örebro, Sweden: Högskolan i Örebro Kvalitetsserien, 1996.

Handal, G. "Etikk i Undervisning og Veiledning" (Ethics in teaching and supervision). In F. Engelstad (ed.), *Etikk i Universitetssamfunnet: Normativ Etikk i Universitetssamfunnet* (Ethics in the university society: Normative ethics in the university society). Oslo: UiO, 1997.

Handal, G., and Lauvås, P. *Promoting Reflective Teaching: Supervision in Action.* Milton Keynes, England: SRHE/Open University Press, 1987.

Hein, P. *Kumbels Lyre.* Copenhagen: Politiken, 1950.

Jordell, K. Ø. *Nasjonal Evaluering av Økonomisk-Administrativ Utdanning: Premisser og Prosess* (National evaluation of economic-administrative education: Premises and process). Oslo: NAVFs Utredningsinstitutt, 1992.

Kierkegaard, S. "Synspunktet for min Forfattervirksomhet: Rapport til Historien" (The view on my activity as an author: Report to history). (Paragraph 2.) *Samlede Verk* (Collected works). Vol. 13. Copenhagen: Nordisk Forlag, 1859.

Lycke, K. H. "Improving Teaching and Practice Through Peer Consultations." Paper presented at the Association for Medical Education in Europe conference "Current Issues in Medical Education," Prague, Sept. 1998.

Murray, H., Gillese, E., Lennon, M., Mercer, P., and Robinson, M. *Ethical Principles in University Teaching.* North York, Ontario: Society for Teaching and Learning in Higher Education, 1996.

NESH (National Committee on Research Ethics for the Social Sciences, Law and Humanities). *Forskningsetiske Retningslinjer for Samfunnsvitenskap, Jus og Humaniora* (Ethical directions for research in the social sciences, law, and humanities). Oslo: NESH, 1994.

Simons, H. *Getting to Know Schools in a Democracy: The Politics and Process of Evaluation.* London: Falmer Press, 1987.

Tiller, T. *Kengurskolen: det Store Spranget* (The kangaroo school: The great leap). Oslo: Gyldendal, 1990.

UiO (University of Oslo). *Yrkesetiske Retningslinjer for Veiledere ved Universitetet i Oslo* (Ethical directions for supervisors at the University of Oslo). Oslo: UiO, 1997.

GUNNAR HANDAL is professor of higher education at the Institute for Educational Research at the University of Oslo, Norway.

8

There is now empirical evidence that consultation with an expert instructional developer has long-term effects on improvement of teaching.

How Individual Consultation Affects Teaching

Sergio Piccinin

There is growing recognition that professionals can benefit from feedback on their practice (Schön, 1983; Erickson, 1986). In the case of higher education, faculty development centers provide a variety of supports for teaching to the faculty they serve. Increasingly, a key service for many teaching centers in North America, if not around the world, is the provision of personal consultation, including feedback, for the improvement of their teaching (Erickson, 1986; Brinko and Menges, 1997; Knapper and others, 1998). Essentially consultation consists of one person, usually a fellow academic, working with another faculty member to deal with instructional problems and improve performance.

Morrison (1997) describes four essential components of instructional consultation. First, consultation must involve a process of reflection on teaching and how it is perceived by others, especially students. Second, consultation is a voluntary activity, carried out for formative (improvement), rather than summative purposes (to gain tenure or promotion). Third, conversations between teacher and consultant occur at various points in the teaching improvement process. Thus, early in the process they might discuss aspects of teaching to be improved and ways of gathering relevant information. Later they would review feedback from the process and discuss specific alternative teaching strategies. Fourth, the entire process takes place in an established time frame, which is arranged on an individual basis between consultant and faculty member.

Morrison also describes a typology of teaching consultation programs and points out some of the advantages and disadvantages of each. In the most common traditional approach, an instructional developer provides assistance on request to an individual faculty member using a variety of techniques for information gathering, analysis, feedback, and follow-up. The consultant typically has extensive knowledge and experience about teaching and learning, possesses a wide repertoire of consultation and facilitation skills, and is employed in the instructional development or teaching center to provide such consultation.

Regardless of the model or approach to instructional consultation, several important research questions arise. Who are the users of such consultation services? Even more important, is such consultation effective in improving teaching and, if so, do the effects persist over time? Clearly these are critical questions. Regardless of how provided, consultation is time consuming and costly. If it is not widely used or ineffective, then it would be unprofessional and irresponsible to offer such a service. The remainder of this chapter is devoted to an examination of issues related to these questions, focusing in particular on my recent study of the uses and impact of individual consultation at a major Canadian university.

Users of Individual Consultation Services

There are few reported studies of who uses individual consultation services (Chism and Szabó, 1997–98; Piccinin and McCoy, 1997; Piccinin, Cristi, and McCoy, in press). In their study on how faculty development programs evaluate their services, Chism and Szabó (1997–98) report that evaluation of consultation services is occasional and inconsistent. Virtually none of the programs included in their study published reports on consultation programs.

Apart from my own study of users of individual consultation at the University of Ottawa, only one other relevant study was found. Stanley, Porter, and Szabó (1996–97) recently conducted a survey of 227 faculty clients described as "consistent users" of teaching centers at two large American research universities. In addition to conducting an assessment of what the authors termed the *developer-client consultation process*, these investigators also provided the first and only comprehensive description of consumers of individual consultation services.

Although their study makes a valuable contribution to our existing knowledge about actual consumers of individual consultation, the sample of consistent users is somewhat problematic. Such users are defined as those who have used individual consultation services more than two times in the preceding five years. But the authors do not specify what constituted a *use*, whether this referred to each interaction separately (such as a telephone conversation, initial interview, class observation) or to one entire consultation process, which may have included one consultation session or many sessions. If the latter, then results of this study would be generalizable only to faculty who seek consultation on a continuing basis. My experience is that although some faculty request consultation on more than one occasion, the majority do not.

What follows is a brief description of users of individual consultation services at a single medium-sized Canadian university over a seven-year period. During this time, I tracked the users of individual consultation to discover their characteristics and how representative they were of the faculty as a whole. I also conducted a study of the effectiveness of the consultation in which they engaged. In total, 165 faculty requested and received some form of individual consultation; 62 percent were male, 38 percent female, a proportion that closely approximates that of the total university faculty (67 percent male and 33 percent female). Most of the sample (115, or 70 percent) were full-time faculty, which is exactly the same as the proportion in the general university population.

Of the full-time faculty seen, 16 percent were full professors, 15 percent associate professors, and the remaining 69 percent assistant professors. In the university as a whole, 36 percent of faculty hold full professor rank, 37 percent are associate professors, and 27 percent are either assistant professors or lecturers. Hence, relative to the total university population, full and associate professors were underrepresented, and assistant professors were overrepresented in the consulting population. The distribution of professors seen according to faculty affiliation closely approximates their proportion in the university.

As to age, the female professors seen ranged from twenty-seven to sixty-one years old, with a mean age of thirty-seven. The age range of male professors seen was from twenty-seven to sixty-two, with a mean of forty-three. The mean ages for the female and male professors seen were somewhat lower than those of the total university population, which are forty-five for females and forty-nine for males. Years of university teaching experience for professors seeking consultation ranged from zero to thirty-three, with a mean of seven years and a median of four years. The latter information was not available for the total university population.

In summary, the data confirm that faculty who sought individual consultation services at the university's teaching center were representative of the larger university faculty in terms of faculty distribution, gender, and full-time or part-time status. On average the faculty seen were somewhat younger and less experienced. This suggests that the consultation services of the teaching center are well known across the campus and are readily accessible to all faculty. Not surprisingly, consultation was more frequently sought by younger, less experienced, nontenured assistant professors. This can be seen as encouraging, because research suggests that faculty are more likely to benefit from intervention early in their careers, rather than later (Diehl and Simpson, 1989). In other words, results from my study indicate that consultation services are being used by faculty most likely to benefit.

This leads to the more fundamental questions concerning teaching consultation. Is such consultation effective? Do the benefits of consultation persist over time? I conducted a study of these questions covering the same seven-year period; the rest of the chapter describes my findings and discusses their implications.

The Impact of Consultation on Teaching

A number of studies have documented the potential effectiveness of consultation on teaching improvement. Cohen (1980), on the basis of his meta-analysis of a number of studies, concluded that feedback from student ratings was much more effective in promoting teaching improvement when used in conjunction with consultation than when student rating information was used alone. These findings were confirmed by Menges and Brinko (1986) in their update of Cohen's analysis, as well as in another major review, by Weimer and Lenze (1991), of efforts to improve university teaching.

However, several authors point to the need for further research to solidify these findings (L'Hommedieu, Menges, and Brinko, 1990; Chism and Szabó, 1997–98). In particular, L'Hommedieu and colleagues conclude their critical meta-analysis with a number of recommendations for further research that focus on important methodological issues. For example, they note that most studies examining the effects of consultation on teaching improvement have used faculty who volunteer to take part in the study rather than the broader population of those who seek help. They recommend the use of larger samples, standardized instruments to measure teaching effectiveness, adequate longitudinal designs, and sampling across subject area and level of teaching experience.

It can be added that there is a dearth of research on the *elements* of individual consultation that might affect teaching. For instance, no research has compared the impact of different forms of individual consultation, yet it is apparent that various consultation processes have been employed across studies. In some cases, for example, consultation consisted of brief meetings between consultant and teacher that focused largely on student ratings and strategies for improvement (Aleamoni, 1978; Overall and Marsh, 1979; McKeachie and others, 1980; Marsh and Roche, 1993). Participants in other studies may have attended workshops in addition to receiving individual consultation (Hoyt and Howard, 1978; Aleamoni and Stevens, 1983; Stevens and Aleamoni, 1985). Other studies additionally incorporated class observation (Wilson, 1986) or videotaping (Erickson and Erickson, 1979; Rozeman and Kerwin, 1991). Clearly, consultation has included a variety of components, some of which may be more strongly linked to teaching improvement than others.

My own study examined the impact of individual consultation on teaching improvement as measured by student ratings, and also addressed the methodological issues raised earlier. It is unique in several ways. First, it is among the first reported studies to examine teaching improvement among actual consumers of teaching consultation services provided by a professional consultant at a university teaching center. Second, the study covers a period of seven academic years, makes use of a larger sample size, and includes faculty representative of all academic areas and levels of experience. Because these faculty are truly representative of those seeking consultation (in other words, they were not recruited for study purposes), the problems they brought to the situation are likely characteristic of the larger population. In addition, the interventions provided by the consultant were jointly determined through faculty-consultant interaction, allowing for a comparative examination of the effects of different types of consultation on teaching improvement.

Study Design. The design of the study was as follows. Of the 165 faculty who consulted the teaching center during the seven-year period, the study sample included only the 91 who sought consultation to improve their teaching in a specific course and for whom complete data (*Pre* and *Post*, as defined below) were available. Individual consultation ranged from a single interview to more intensive interventions involving one or more of the following: class observation, videotaping of lectures, consultation with students, and feedback from the consultant. Not all faculty sought or received identical consultation services from the teaching center. Interventions by the consultant, based on the request of the teacher or negotiated between teacher and consultant, fell into these categories.

1. *Feedback-Consultation (FC: 31 Cases).* Intervention for this category typically consisted of one interview in which the consultant engaged in a discussion with the professor concerning issues that the latter wished to raise related to the improvement of teaching in a specific course.

2. *Feedback-Consultation-Class Observation (FCO: 19 Cases).* This category consisted of feedback and consultation as described above, but also included observation of the professor's class followed by one or more sessions that offered detailed feedback and suggestions for teaching in a specific course.

3. *Feedback-Consultation-Class Observation-Student Feedback (FCOS: 41 Cases).* In addition to the interventions provided in the FCO category, the FCOS intervention incorporated, at the professor's request, direct student feedback obtained by the consultant during a private session with the professor's students.

The measure of teaching effectiveness was a standardized student rating form that is regularly used at the University of Ottawa: it is administered to students at the end of each term in every course and across all departments. The results are publicly accessible and published yearly. Students rate teaching and courses for twelve items on a scale ranging from 1 (poor) to 5 (excellent). The items deal with course organization, workload, marking of tests and assignments, feedback provided on learning progress, professor's knowledge of subject matter, ability to convey the subject matter effectively, teacher's preparation, ability to stimulate interest, rapport with the class, availability, plus two general ratings of the course and the teacher. A mean score is reported for each item. For the purpose of this study two means were calculated. The first was an overall mean for all twelve items. The second was a combined mean for three items: the general rating of the professor as a teacher, the item on effectiveness at conveying subject matter, and the item that measured teacher preparation.

The study examined student ratings of the individual's teaching of the same course at four points: one to three years prior to consultation (Pre 1), at the time of consultation (Pre 2), at the end of the semester or year after the consultation (Post 1), and one to three years after the consultation (Post 2). To test whether consultation improved teaching performance, end-of-semester student ratings for the relevant course (Post 1 ratings) were compared with student ratings for the same course at the time consultation was sought (Pre 2). To examine whether any effects of consultation persisted over time, Post 1 student ratings were compared to student ratings for that same course taught by the professor from one to three years following consultation (Post 2). To be included in the sample for this comparison, professors must have had available both Pre 2 data and Post 2 data for the course that was the subject of the consultation. Of the ninety-one professors who had both Post 1 data and Pre 2 data, eighty also had Post 2 data. This reduced the sample size in each intervention category to twenty-eight in the FC group, sixteen in the FCO group, and thirty-six in the FCOS group. Nonetheless, the number of subjects in the present study is the largest sample to date in which teaching improvement following consultation has been studied, and affords sufficient statistical power to yield valid results.

In order to afford a valid control measure and ensure that changes in student ratings were in fact a consequence of the consultation intervention, and not time effects, the Pre 2 data were compared with Pre 1 data. In other words, a comparison was made between student ratings for the course at the time of consultation, and student ratings for the same course taught one to three years prior to the consultation. Because control data were not available for all ninety-one professors the sample size for the control comparison was reduced to seventy-three, with twenty-five in the FC group, fourteen in the FCO group, and thirty-four in the FCOS group.

Results. Only the highlights of the results are presented briefly here. For a more detailed analysis see Piccinin, Cristi, and McCoy (in press). First some demographic data are presented, followed by an analysis of the control comparison, and finally the main analysis of the changes in teacher ratings.

Demographic Data. As was the case with the sample seeking consultation described earlier, this group of ninety-one faculty closely resembled the university population in terms of gender and full- or part-time status. Relative to the population of full-time faculty, full and associate professors were underrepresented, while assistant professors were overrepresented. Faculty affiliation was very similar to that of the university as a whole. In general the demographics of the three consultation groups (FC, FCO, and FCOS) follow the same pattern.

Student Ratings of Instruction: Control Comparison. In order to obtain a control comparison and to ensure that any observable teaching improvements were not merely an artifact of time, the mean student course ratings at the time of consultation (Pre 2) were compared with the mean student ratings for the same or a similar course (Pre 1) taught in a previous year. Mean student ratings were subjected to a two (evaluation time: Pre 1 versus Pre 2) by three (consultation group: FC, FCO, and FCOS) ANOVA, with the evaluation time as a repeated measure, and consultation group as a between-subject factor. These analyses were conducted for the mean overall student ratings, for the mean student ratings of each of the twelve items, and for the mean combined student ratings of three key items used by the university in assessing candidates for tenure and promotion. Eighteen professors from the initial sample of ninety-one had to be dropped for this analysis because they had no Pre 1 data available.

The overall mean ratings on the twelve-item rating form are presented in Table 8.1 and Figure 8.1. No differences were found between the Pre 1 course and the Pre 2 course mean student ratings for either the twelve items or for the combined items used for tenure and promotion decisions. Thus any change in student ratings post consultation could reasonably be attributable to consultation effects and not to time effects.

Student Ratings of Instruction: Main Statistical Analysis. All mean student ratings were then submitted to a two (evaluation time) by three (consultation group) ANOVA, with evaluation time as a repeated measure and consultation group as a between-subject factor. In all comparisons, the analyses were conducted for the mean overall student rating, for the mean student rating of each of the twelve items, and for the mean student rating of three combined items.

The overall mean ratings are presented in Table 8.1 and Figure 8.1. Statistically significant differences (<.01) were found between the mean Pre 2 and Post 1 student ratings of instruction for the FCO and FCOS groups, but not for the FC group. The same pattern emerged when the Pre 2 and Post 1 ratings were compared on the means of the three items used in tenure and promotion procedures. These findings indicate that teaching improved as indicated by the increase in overall student rating following FCO and FCOS consultation but not following FC consultation.

Comparison of the Post 1 and Post 2 overall mean student ratings yielded no significant differences for the FCO and FCOS groups, but in the case of the FC group the difference was significant. Again this same pattern emerged for the three combined scales. This indicates that the gains in student ratings following the consultation process (as measured by an improvement in student ratings at Post 1) were maintained at follow-up for the FCO and FCOS groups. Interestingly, members of the FC group, who showed no measurable initial benefits from consultation, did demonstrate a significant improvement in their teaching at Post 2. In other words, there seems to be a delayed improvement for the FC group.

Discussion. The study reported here examined the users of an individual teaching consultation service provided by a teaching center and the impact of this consultation on teaching improvement as measured by student ratings. This research is unique in that it involves the largest number of participants for a study of this type and for the fact that users were genuine and typical

**Table 8.1. Overall Student Ratings Across Time
in the Three Consultation Groups**

Evaluation Time		Consultation Group		
		FC	FCO	FCOS
Pre 1 (n = 73)	n	25	14	34
	Mean	3.88	3.67	3.46
	S.D.	(.402)	(.512)	(.407)
Pre 2 (n = 91)	n	31	19	41
	Mean	3.81	3.68	3.44
	S.D.	(.440)	(.503)	(.422)
Post 1 (n = 91)	n	31	19	41
	Mean	3.77	4.01	3.71
	S.D.	(.491)	(.373)	(.422)
Post 2 (n = 80)	n	28	16	36
	Mean	4.05	3.85	3.75
	S.D.	(.380)	(.257)	(.365)

Note: FC intervention consisted of feedback and consultation; FCO intervention consisted of feedback, consultation, and class observation; FCOS intervention consisted of feedback, consultation, class observation, and student feedback.

clients of the teaching center as opposed to specially recruited volunteers. The group was also characteristic of teachers at the university in terms of gender, faculty affiliation, and full- or part-time status. Participants were also generally representative in terms of rank and range of teaching experience.

This strengthens the credibility and generalizability of the findings by reducing the likelihood that any observed teaching improvements were a function of the sample. It should be noted that although some of those seen have been teaching for almost thirty years, approximately two-thirds in all three intervention groups had less than ten years' experience. At the same time, it is interesting to note that almost 20 percent of those who by choice received the fullest, most intensive intervention (FCOS) are professors who have been teaching more than twenty years. Also of interest is an apparent anomaly in the male-female balance. About half the FC group are females, but only one quarter of the FCO and FCOS groups are females. Why females tended to select the least intrusive intervention is not readily explained.

Another strength of this study is the evidence provided by the control comparison. The absence of any difference between the Pre 2 and Pre 1 course mean student ratings implies that any change in ratings following consultation can reasonably be attributed to the effects of the consultation itself and not just to the passage of time. The fact that this authentic group of teachers selected different levels of consultation made it possible to exam-

Figure 8.1. Comparison of Overall Mean Student Ratings Across Time for the Three Consultation Groups

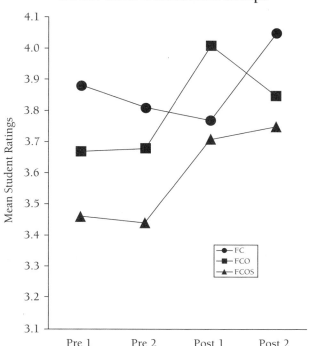

ine the outcomes from three different intensities of consultation—yet another unique aspect of the present study.

The results showed clearly that consultation was effective in improving the quality of teaching as measured by increased mean student ratings of instruction. Furthermore, follow-up testing (Post 2) indicates that this effect persisted for one to three years after the consultation. The results are consistent with previous research showing both the positive and long-lasting effects of consultation on teaching performance (Mahler and Benor, 1984; Aleamoni and Stevens, 1983; Stevens and Aleamoni, 1985; Erickson, 1986; Wilson, 1986; Sheets and Henry, 1988). The present findings, however, significantly extend our understanding of the effects of consultation because teaching improvement was examined among actual consumers of consultation services and because the sample of professors studied is the largest to date.

It is interesting to note that the three groups receiving consultation differed significantly in their preconsultation student ratings. More specifically, groups with lower prior student ratings opted for more intense interventions. The FC group represented the least intensive intervention and had the highest preconsultation mean ratings, while the FCOS group received the most intensive intervention and had the lowest preconsultation ratings. It seems logical that through self-selection and discussion with the consultant, those with the highest preconsultation student evaluations would request and receive the least intensive interventions and those with the lowest ratings would receive the most intensive interventions. This appears to be what happened.

Teaching improved as measured by an increase in overall student rating at Post 1, following FCO and FCOS consultation, but not following FC consultation. Thus change was seen immediately after the intervention except in the case of brief consultation. The Post 2 data, however, revealed a significant increase in teaching performance for the FC group, pointing to the utility of this intervention approach. It appears that even brief consultation can lead to statistically significant change in teaching effectiveness.

Why the FC group, which showed no significant initial gains after consultation, demonstrated improved teaching performance at Post 2 warrants discussion. The FC group started with higher student ratings so that there was less room for members of this group to change, particularly to show statistically significant improvement. In addition, the intervention for this group was the least intensive in the sense that it typically consisted of one meeting to discuss teaching as opposed to also including classroom observation and further feedback. A somewhat larger proportion of faculty in this group (29 percent) taught part-time and therefore may have had less opportunity to integrate suggestions for change into their teaching. Those seen for brief consultation were least in need, as evidenced by their higher preconsultation ratings than the other groups. Consequently, they may have felt a less pressing need to make changes. Finally, it could be that given their already better preconsultation ratings, any improvement for this group is not as readily perceived by students. Further research is needed to ascertain why FC interventions resulted in a delayed effect on teaching improvement. Certainly the finding of a delayed effect clearly points to the importance of tracking change in teaching performance over time, as suggested by L'Hommedieu and others (1990). The follow-up data for the FCO and FCOS groups demonstrated that the teaching improvement acquired through consultation was well maintained over time.

Because the university uses three particular items from the rating scale in making tenure and promotion decisions, it was possible here to investigate whether individual consultation led to improvement on these specific scales. This is important from the consumer perspective because faculty applying for tenure are more likely to seek consultation. It was found that the pattern of results for the three key items closely mirrored the pattern observed for the overall mean student ratings on all twelve scales. This lends support to the practice of providing consultation services to faculty who plan to apply for contract renewal, tenure, or promotion.

Although self-reports from faculty were not systematically gathered, the consultant has received unsolicited positive feedback from a large number of people on the improvement in their student ratings and, more important, about increased self-confidence, feelings of competence, and teaching satisfaction following consultation. In other words, the statistical findings are supported by informal and anecdotal data.

Conclusion

These findings confirm the effectiveness of using consultation to help faculty improve their overall teaching performance. Even brief consultation can result in statistically significant and meaningful teaching improvement. Furthermore, the results show that positive effects persisted for one to three years after the consultation took place. Future research might examine how long the positive effects of consultation persist and what effects (if any) booster sessions might have.

The postconsultation data clearly point to the efficacy of all three types of consultation described here. However, it is clear that intervention approaches differentially affect teaching improvement. All interventions significantly improved teaching performance, with brief consultation having a delayed but no less perceptible effect. Although this delayed effect needs to be better understood, the results as a whole point to the appropriateness of using different consultation approaches based on the needs of the individual teacher. There is no way of knowing what would have been the effect of using the same intervention for all groups. Future research should address the question of what type of intervention is best suited for different populations, as well as what style of consultation is most effective in promoting maximum change.

Replication of these findings is needed to increase the generalizability of findings beyond the present sample. The impact of varied approaches and methods used by different consultants may also become clearer as other centers conduct similar studies. Additional studies would also be important for comparative purposes. In particular, future research could address the effects of consultation tailored for specific needs. Centers could share information about the types of interventions that have been successful in bringing about teaching improvement. It is plausible that this would reduce the amount of trial and error, particularly for newly created centers.

Clearly there is much to be learned from continued research on the effects of consultation services. In particular, the evaluation of educational development programs is important for strengthening their work and ultimately for enhancing the quality of teaching in our institutions of higher learning.

References

Aleamoni, L. A. "The Usefulness of Student Evaluations in Improving College Teaching." *Instructional Science,* 1978, 7, 95–105.

Aleamoni, L., and Stevens, J. "The Effectiveness of Consultation in Support of Student Evaluation Feedback: A Ten-Year Follow-Up." Paper presented at the annual meeting of the Rocky Mountain Psychological Association, Albuquerque, N.M., Apr.–May 1983.

Brinko, K. T., and Menges, R. J. (eds.). *Practically Speaking: A Sourcebook for Instructional Consultants in Higher Education.* Stillwater, Okla.: New Forums Press, 1997.

Chism, V.N.N., and Szabó, B. "How Faculty Development Programs Evaluate Their Services." *Journal of Staff, Program, and Organization Development,* 1997–98, *15* (2), 55–62.

Cohen, P. A. "Effectiveness of Student-Rating Feedback for Improving College Instruction: A Meta-Analysis of Findings." *Research in Higher Education,* 1980, *13,* 321–341.

Diehl, P. F., and Simpson, R. D. "Investing in Junior Faculty: The Teaching Improvement Program (TIPS)." *Innovative Higher Education,* 1989, *13* (2), 147–157.

Erickson, G. R. "A Survey of Faculty Development Practices." In *To Improve the Academy,* 1986, *5,* 182–196.

Erickson, G. R., and Erickson, B. L. "Improving College Teaching." *Journal of Higher Education,* 1979, *50,* 670–683.

Hoyt, D. P., and Howard, G. S. "The Evaluation of Faculty Development Programs." *Research in Higher Education,* 1978, *8,* 25–38.

Knapper, C., Piccinin, S., Millis, B., Beaty, E., and Hicks, O. "Instructional Consultation: International Perspectives." Paper presented at the International Consortium for Educational Development conference, Austin, Tex., Apr. 1998.

L'Hommedieu, R., Menges, R. J., and Brinko, K. T. "Methodological Explanations for the Modest Effects of Feedback from Student Ratings." *Journal of Educational Psychology,* 1990, *82* (2), 232–241.

Mahler, S., and Benor, D. E. "Short- and Long-Term Effects of a Teacher-Training Workshop in Medical School." *Higher Education,* 1984, *13,* 265–273.

Marsh, H. W., and Roche, L. "The Use of Students' Evaluations and an Individually Structured Intervention to Enhance University Teaching Effectiveness." *American Educational Research Journal,* 1993, *30* (1), 217–251.

McKeachie, W. J., Lin, Y. G., Daugherty, M., Moffet, M. M., Neigler, C., Nork, N. J., Walz, M., and Baldwin, R. "Using Student Ratings and Consultation to Improve Instruction." *British Journal of Educational Psychology,* 1980, *50,* 168–174.

Menges, R. J., and Brinko, K. T. "Effects of Student Evaluation Feedback: A Meta-Analysis of Higher Education Research." Paper presented at the 71st annual meeting of the American Educational Research Association, Washington, D.C., Apr. 1986.

Morrison, D. E. "Overview of Instructional Consultation in North America." In K. T. Brinko and R. J. Menges (eds.), *Practically Speaking: A Sourcebook for Instructional Consultants in Higher Education.* Stillwater, Okla.: New Forums Press, 1997.

Overall, J. U., and Marsh, H. W. "Midterm Feedback from Students: Its Relationship to Instructional Improvement and Students' Cognitive and Affective Outcomes." *Journal of Educational Psychology,* 1979, *71,* 856–865.

Piccinin, S., Cristi, C., and McCoy, M. "The Impact of Individual Consultation on Student Ratings of Teaching." *International Journal for Academic Development,* in press.

Piccinin, S., and McCoy, M. *Consumers of Individual Consultation Services Offered to Professors at a University Teaching Center: A Descriptive Study.* Ottawa: University of Ottawa, 1997.

Rozeman, J. E., and Kerwin, M. A. "Evaluating the Effectiveness of a Teaching Consultation Program on Changing Student Ratings of Teaching Behaviors." *Journal of Staff, Program, and Organization Development,* 1991, *9* (4), 223–230.

Schön, D. A. *The Reflective Practitioner: How Professionals Think in Action.* New York: Basic Books, 1983.

Sheets, K. J., and Henry, R. C. "Evaluation of a Faculty Development Program for Family Physicians." *Medical Teacher,* 1988, *10,* 75–83.

Stanley, C. A., Porter, M. E., and Szabó, B. L. "An Exploratory Study of the Faculty Developer–Client Relationship." *Journal of Staff, Program, and Organization Development,* 1996–97, *14* (3), 115–126.

Stevens, J., and Aleamoni, L. "The Use of Evaluative Feedback for Instructional Improvement: A Longitudinal Perspective." *Instructional Science,* 1985, *13,* 285–304.

Weimer, M., and Lenze, L. F. "Instructional Interventions: A Review of the Literature on Efforts to Improve Instruction." In J. Smart (ed.), *Higher Education: Handbook of Theory and Research.* New York: Agathon Press, 1991.

Wilson, R. C. "Improving Faculty Teaching: Effective Use of Student Evaluations and Consultants." *Journal of Higher Education,* 1986, *57* (2), 196–211.

SERGIO PICCININ is professor of psychology and director of the Centre for University Teaching at the University of Ottawa, Canada.

Moving toward an integrated approach to instructional consultation has implications for faculty, the teaching and learning center, and the institution as a whole.

Toward an Integrated Approach to Instructional Consultation

Cynthia Weston, Lynn McAlpine

Consultation to improve teaching in higher education institutions takes many different forms. But Gibbs (1996) summarizes the situation well when he says that much instructional development activity (which for us includes instructional consultation) "is organized and undertaken centrally by centrally funded and managed units and staff; it is often generic rather than discipline-specific and targeted on individuals rather than on departments" (p. 27). This centralized generic approach is perceived by some as problematic because the primary allegiance of most faculty members is to their discipline (see, for example, Jenkins, 1996). Many of us who are concerned with teaching development in higher education (including Gibbs and Jenkins) now believe that if we are to have a significant impact on enhancing teaching, then consultation should also come from within academic departments or units and should focus on discipline-based concerns.

In this chapter we discuss an expansion of our approach to instructional consultation at our Centre for University Teaching and Learning (CUTL) from a primarily central generic model to an approach that tries to integrate more discipline-based concerns and have more department and faculty involvement. We focus on (1) factors that underlie our desire to change our approach, (2) our goals and strategies, and (3) the implications for faculty members and the institution. Professors and others who contribute to enhancing university teaching may find this discussion provides a basis for being more intentional about their own work in teaching development. But first, we provide what we believe is a useful way of analyzing and classifying any instructional consultation.

Analyzing Elements of a Consultation

By *instructional consultation* we mean all activities that are carried out for the purpose of enhancing teaching at the university, for example giving a workshop, participating in policymaking, meeting with professors. This definition—any intervention that provides guidance related to teaching— may be a bit broader than the definitions used in other chapters, but we think it provides formal recognition of the many university activities that take place to improve teaching. For us, a consultant may be a member of a teaching and learning center or another professor who has both interest and expertise in teaching and takes on a visible role in instructional consultation.

What aspects of instructional consultation might change when moving from a primarily central generic approach to incorporate more discipline-based concerns and more departmental and faculty involvement? Hicks (1998) provides a two-dimensional matrix for analyzing teaching development activities that has helped us think about what might change. One dimension of his matrix represents the nature of the teaching development activity as generic or discipline-specific; the other dimension represents the source of responsibility for the activity as central or local. Teaching development activities can be located in one of the four quadrants formed by these two dimensions, based on differences in the nature of the activity and responsibility.

We found this characterization useful and have delineated factors that we believe further explain variation in each dimension. Differences inherent in the central-local dimension can be further explained by considering (1) the consultant's home base, (2) the ownership and responsibility for the consultation, and (3) the level for which the consultation is designed. Differences in the generic versus discipline-specific dimension can be further defined in terms of (4) the consultant's perspective on teaching and learning, and (5) the concerns that drive the consultation.

For the central-local dimension, the consultant's home (as defined by the nature of the appointment, who pays the salary, and the primary focus of work) might reside in a centrally funded and managed teaching development center or locally in a department or faculty. Similarly, the ownership and responsibility for initiating, organizing, and implementing the consultation could lie with the central teaching development center or with a local unit such as a department or faculty. The level for which the consultation is designed can be central, such as university-wide workshops on teaching portfolios, or local, as in the case of faculty-level portfolio workshops that help interpret university requirements in light of local promotion practices.

In terms of the generic versus discipline-specific dimension, the consultant's perspective on teaching and learning might be generic, derived from universal principles of teaching and learning (for instance, based on principles from educational psychology or instructional design), or based on and contextualized in a discipline-specific perspective, related to the structure of the subject matter. Likewise, the concerns that drive the consultation could be generic issues that are relevant across disciplines, such as teaching large classes, or more discipline-specific concerns, such as matching the nature of the subject matter to be learned to the most appropriate instructional strategies.

Performing an analysis of instructional consultations in relation to these elements helps us to recognize changes in roles, responsibilities, and perspectives, and to be intentional in selecting approaches. These elements of instructional consultation are revisited throughout the discussion of our goals and strategies; in the Conclusion we return to the elements that have and will change.

Factors Underlying Our Expanded Approach

McGill University's Centre for University Teaching and Learning was established in 1969 and is centrally funded by the vice principal (academic). Up to ten years ago CUTL's approach to instructional consultation could be characterized as mostly central and generic. CUTL organized, implemented, and often initiated instructional consultations. The concerns driving consultations tended to be generic, such as teaching large classes or grading. Subsequently, CUTL began to include a more discipline-specific orientation by designing consultations for particular departments or faculties, and incorporating applications relevant to their needs. Several conceptual and contextual factors influenced our decision to expand our instructional consultation to include more local responsibility and a more discipline-based perspective. These included beliefs about how teaching improvement occurs, the importance of discipline-based approaches, and contextual factors such as reduced resources and increased demand for educational development services.

Teaching Improvement as a Conceptual Change Process. We and others have come to understand the evolution of expertise in teaching as a complex process requiring experimentation, practice, feedback, and reflection over time (Ramsden, 1992; Saroyan, Amundsen, and Li, 1997; Kember, 1997; Ho, 1998). Teaching development can be seen as progressing through a series of increasingly sophisticated stages that are characterized by conceptual changes in the way the professor thinks about how learning takes place, how to structure the content for learning, and how student and instructor interact in this process.

Our beliefs about how teaching improvement occurs have caused us to move away from short-term interventions such as one-time workshops and other brief events. These may generate interest and promote initial enthusiasm but do little to help instructors develop an overall understanding of the teaching and learning process or to make thoughtful and informed decisions about learning goals and teaching strategies (see Weimer and Lenze, 1994; Murray, 1997). Because the development of teaching expertise requires that professors have opportunities to experiment, practice, receive feedback, and reflect on what they have done, we have moved toward longer consultations designed to allow the necessary time, guidance, and support to foster conceptual change.

Discipline-Specific Applications as Situated Learning. The notion that teaching expertise develops over time, coupled with our belief that learning about teaching is more effective if it is situated and contextualized (Shulman, 1987; Laurillard, 1993) led us to include discipline-specific applications in some of our consultations. We have learned that generic principles are understood and implemented much more readily when they have been contextualized and situated through immediate application to the teacher's own situation. This process is also effective in fostering conceptual change in the way professors think about teaching and learning (Saroyan, Amundsen, and Li, 1997).

The primary example in our institution of a longer intervention designed to foster discipline-based conceptual change is our course design and teaching consultation in which a group of twenty-four professors from a variety of departments are brought together each year for a weeklong (forty-hour) intensive workshop. Each professor designs or redesigns a course (or program or curriculum) of his or her choice. Professors begin the process by creating a map of the course's major concepts to represent graphically their understanding of the concepts and structure of knowledge in the course. They then work through a process of defining what the students should learn about each concept (learning outcomes), how they should guide and facilitate learning to achieve each outcome (instructional strategies), and how to assess whether the desired learning has been achieved (evaluation of learning). Feedback is provided by peers and consultants at each stage. In this way teachers learn about the generic principles of course design (content, outcomes, teaching strategies, and evaluation) by contextualizing and applying them to the planning of their own course. Concurrently the professors take part in a series of microteaching sessions, in which they practice teaching to the group several segments of the course they are designing, with feedback again given by peers and consultants.

The facilitators in this process are a combination of CUTL staff and professors from different faculties who have previously participated in the course design workshop. These consultants from the disciplines are important contributors to the process because they interpret generic principles in a meaningful way for their colleagues. The consultation begins with the basics of instructional design that the participants over time, and with practice, feedback, and reflection, contextualize and apply to a meaningful project within their own disciplines.

Contextual Factors. Several contextual factors have also influenced our expanded approach to instructional consultation. These include the nature of the institution, results of a recent cyclical review, and advice from a teaching and learning committee.

McGill is a research-intensive university in which there is great pressure to have active funded research programs. This can make it difficult for some faculty members to focus on teaching. McGill is also decentralized, which means that many policies, such as mandatory course evaluations, can be (and are!) implemented differently by each department. In this context it is challenging to communicate and coordinate university-wide activities. In addition, like many other universities, McGill has undergone crippling budget cuts over the past ten years: faculty who leave are often not replaced, new appointments are few and far between, and early retirements are encouraged.

CUTL underwent a cyclical review in 1995–96 that caused us to rethink our approach to teaching development and our relationship with other units on campus. As part of the process we articulated our interest in expanding instructional consultation from a centralized generic approach to include more local activity. This change in approach required faculties and departments to take on increased responsibility, allowed teaching development to be designed with the particular concerns and values of the discipline in mind, and was targeted directly to achieve departmental strategic goals. We anticipated that increased ownership and responsibility for teaching development by academic units would also increase dialogue about teaching, making it a more valued component of the McGill community of scholarship. Our interest in changing and expanding our approach was supported and it was recommended that the Subcommittee on University Teaching and Learning (SCUTL) take a more active role in teaching development at McGill.

SCUTL was established in 1987 for the purpose of advising the university on issues related to teaching and learning. It is chaired by the vice principal (academic), has representation from every faculty, and counts the director of CUTL as a standing member. The Subcommittee studies development needs and makes recommendations on university policy related to enhancement of teaching and learning. Examples of such policies are mandatory course evaluations (1980) and use of teaching portfolios as a mandatory part of tenure and promotion (1994). The recommendation from the cyclical review that SCUTL become more active gave us an idea for expanding our approach to instructional consultation; this strategy is discussed in the next section.

Expanding Our Teaching Development Approach

Our approach to instructional consultation in recent years has been a mix of central generic consultations and an increasing number of discipline-specific consultations including departmental curriculum reviews facilitated by CUTL consultants. In addition there have been a few local activities in which CUTL has been only indirectly involved, such as the teaching development committee established in the Faculty of Engineering by a professor who has regularly participated in CUTL events. And just this year a university-wide discussion group on teaching was initiated and implemented by a professor from the Faculty of Education.

Goal: An Integrated Approach. As these initiatives took root we began to anticipate problems with uncontrolled growth, in particular the possibility of duplication, lack of coordination, and absence of quality control. We realized that our goal was to achieve what Hicks (1998) calls an integrated approach to instructional consultation: one that includes all central-local and generic versus discipline-specific combinations of consultations, but—most important—has these consultations connected and coordinated through a collaborative process for maximum impact.

We currently envision a network of CUTL faculty associates, ideally with one consultant in each faculty (and perhaps eventually in most departments), funded by the unit concerned. We have been particularly influenced by DeZure's ideas (1995), and have based some of our thinking about the formation of teaching development consultants on her *faculty liaison* model. The role of faculty associates would be, in collaboration with CUTL, to help their units take ownership and responsibility for teaching development and to serve as liaisons between the units and CUTL. In this way development can be expanded to benefit a greater number of faculty members, and at the same time, needs and strategic goals within units can be identified, and teaching development can be interpreted and delivered from a disciplinary perspective.

Strategies. We are currently using four strategies that take advantage of existing structures and human resources to build a network of faculty associates. Regardless of the strategy, we realize the importance of building a common language and shared knowledge base with the associates to ensure continuity and quality. This will be handled differently for each strategy.

SCUTL Members. The first strategy focuses on developing members of SCUTL as faculty associates. Taking a cue from the recommendation that SCUTL become more active, in September 1997 we proposed that the role of Subcommittee members be gradually shifted to that of associates. In order to fulfill this role, we arranged to use a portion of the SCUTL meetings for building and exchange of knowledge to prepare members to work more directly within their units to foster or initiate instructional consultation. Thus every SCUTL meeting in 1997–98 included an interactive workshop (at the first meeting a two-hour event, later thirty minutes) dealing with critical issues in teaching and learning as well as discussion of ways members could create, implement, and sustain teaching development activities in their own faculties.

After surveying SCUTL members to find out what topics were of most interest, we developed one workshop for each meeting of the academic year. The first described the rationale underlying the CUTL approach to teaching development and introduced the course design and teaching process. The second workshop focused on the nature of student learning and how to evaluate it. The third dealt with the evaluation of teaching; the fourth with assessing and addressing teaching development needs. In the fifth workshop three professors presented case studies on how they themselves had initiated instructional consultation in philosophy, history, and engineering. At the final meeting, the vice principal summarized the events of the year and suggested future directions. Among his suggestions for 1998–99 were that the deans be systematically invited to SCUTL to discuss what is being done to enhance teaching in their respective faculties.

During the current year (1998–99) the interactive sessions are continuing, and groups of committee members are being formed to work collaboratively in identifying teaching development projects for their own faculties to implement in 1999–2000. The location of SCUTL meetings is being rotated through different faculties; the respective deans are invited to talk about local teaching development projects. Faculty members are also invited to attend. The deans have been asked to support creation of faculty associates by recommending professors who are seen as teaching leaders. They have also been asked to provide a formal mechanism for their SCUTL representative to communicate both to the Subcommittee and the faculty, and help overcome the communication problems that are inherent at McGill. Communication within the network of faculty associates is crucial to the success of an integrated program.

Royal Bank Faculty Associates. A second strategy uses a different approach for developing faculty associates. In September 1997 we suggested that funds from an existing grant be rechanneled to establish the Royal Bank Faculty Associate in University Teaching. Through an annual competition, a grant of $6,000 is available to support a McGill professor to work with CUTL on a faculty or department teaching development project proposed by the applicant. The time commitment is expected to be equivalent to one course in each semester, and the knowledge base is developed through a one-year apprenticeship with a member of the CUTL staff with similar interests.

Deans are asked to support this strategy in several ways. First, a faculty must provide evidence of an applicant's leadership in teaching. Further, a letter from the dean must explain the value of the proposed project to the faculty. If there is more than one applicant from a faculty, deans are encouraged to consider the relative impact of the different proposals in light of their priorities. Finally, the faculty must show financial support for the project by providing a $6,000 matching contribution. In these ways the faculty associate and the faculty administration begin to take ownership and responsibility for local teaching development.

The first Royal Bank Faculty Associate, a professor from the Faculty of Engineering, began his project in September 1998. He is developing a Web-based version of the CUTL course design and teaching workshop for engineering professors. Each year the network of Royal Bank Faculty Associates will grow.

Shared Appointment Between a Faculty and CUTL. A third strategy for developing faculty associates is through joint appointments. All CUTL staff have appointments in the Faculty of Education, and this year a part-time professor in the center has a shared appointment with the Faculty of Medicine. CUTL has found that this relationship creates synergy, because we are made more aware of the interests and needs of the Faculty of Medicine and it is easier to find ways to collaborate and link activities.

CUTL is now in the process of replacing a position. We believe that a similar partnership with another faculty would be productive and have agreement with the Faculties of Engineering (25 percent) and Science (50 percent) for shared positions. The individuals will have homes in both our center and the relevant department and will be selected jointly by CUTL and the faculty. The appointees will have an academic background in higher education as well as in their disciplines to ensure the necessary knowledge base and generic perspective on teaching and learning issues. The strategy of shared appointments has several benefits for developing an integrated program of instructional consultation, including improved communication, liaison, and availability at the local level of an instructional development consultant.

Volunteer Contributors. A fourth strategy involves recognizing as teaching development consultants the large group of individual professors who have participated in CUTL activities over time and frequently volunteer to support teaching development. In effect, these professors have undertaken an apprenticeship they have initiated. At the institutional level their contribution, which is vital to our effectiveness, has taken the form of leading small groups and making presentations at centrally organized workshops, where they bring a unique disciplinary perspective on teaching and learning issues. At the local level they have made many contributions, such as setting up teaching committees in their own departments.

We already regard these people as informal teaching development consultants. We are now seeking ways to recognize their efforts and offer them more formal roles as faculty associates. We have asked deans to consider strategies for directing the enthusiasm of these volunteer contributors in ways that can formally support teaching development goals in their units.

What Changes in an Integrated Approach?

Earlier we asked what aspects of instructional consultation will change as we expand from a primarily central approach to more integrated instructional consultation. Such an expansion does not alter some of our fundamental perspectives on teaching and learning, in particular that teaching expertise grows through a conceptual development process situated within the discipline. But we do see changes in many aspects of the central-local and generic versus discipline-specific dimensions on Hicks's matrix (1998).

Consultants will no longer be exclusively located in the central unit but will also work out of their home faculty for most or part of the time.

Responsibility for instructional development will move along a continuum from central control to faculty ownership, and the level for which consultations are designed will involve an increasing number of programs for local units. The concerns driving consultations and consultants' own perspectives on teaching and learning will expand from being primarily generic to an increasing focus on local issues.

What is the role of a teaching and learning center in such an integrated program? The mandate of CUTL within the university remains the same. In particular, CUTL staff will continue to conduct research on the improvement of university teaching and learning, and participate in the development of university policy affecting all faculty. In the case of instructional consultations, CUTL members will continue to run generic central programs where appropriate, but increasingly they will shift efforts to work in reciprocal partnership with faculty associates to build discipline-specific programs and create a shared knowledge base. Overall, CUTL will be centrally responsible for program integration and for ensuring that the activities of all teaching development consultants are linked and coherent so as to make a cumulative impact on improving teaching and learning at McGill.

Implications of an Integrated Program

An integrated program of instructional consultation has implications for faculty members and for the institution as a whole.

Faculty Members. First, an integrated program provides the opportunity to recognize the many contributions of volunteer faculty by formally incorporating them into the network of teaching development consultants. Further, in an integrated approach the role of faculty in teaching development will be transformed as they increasingly take primary responsibility for initiating, designing, and implementing instructional consultation in their units. At least initially this will require substantial time and commitment, as individual professors serve first in an apprenticeship role and later as consultants for their departments. This work must somehow be recognized and rewarded by the institution (more about this later). Finally, we see a benefit for all teaching development consultants, those from CUTL and those from faculties, as they learn from each other, share their knowledge about teaching, and develop new skills (McAlpine and Harris, 1999).

Institution. At the institutional level, there will be a shift in aspects of ownership and responsibility for teaching development from CUTL to the faculties. Faculty ownership implies commitment of resources, such as providing faculty time, money, and rewards for instructional consultation and initiatives in general. Moreover, faculties will have to take the initiative in identifying local teaching needs, creating teaching development plans, and then organizing, implementing, and evaluating the instructional consultations they provide.

The most urgent requirement is that the institution create appropriate rewards and recognition for teaching development consultants. It must be clear to faculty members that attention to teaching is truly valued at the university if they are to devote precious time to working with colleagues. At present, work on teaching development is often rewarded by granting release time from teaching itself. We wonder about the message conveyed regarding the value of teaching when the responsibility from which professors are freed is teaching *load*. To communicate the value of teaching in the university, rewards must be evident in the standards for hiring, tenure, promotion, and merit.

The most important benefit to the institution of an integrated program is the development of a community of scholarship around teaching (Boyer, 1990; Edgerton, Hutchings, and Quinlan, 1991; Shulman, 1993). As faculty ownership increases, the dialogue about teaching within the disciplines will also grow, thus bringing teaching truly into the community of scholarship.

References

Boyer, E. *Scholarship Reconsidered: Priorities of the Professoriate.* Princeton, N.J.: The Carnegie Foundation for the Advancement of Teaching, 1990.

DeZure, D. *Moving Instructional Development Closer to the Disciplines.* Paper presented at the national conference of the American Association for Higher Education, Washington, D.C., Mar. 1995.

Edgerton, R., Hutchings, P., and Quinlan, K. *The Teaching Portfolio: Capturing the Scholarship in Teaching.* Washington, D.C.: American Association for Higher Education, 1991.

Gibbs, G. "Supporting Educational Development Within Departments." *International Journal for Academic Development,* 1996, *1,* 27–37.

Hicks, O. "Integration of Central and Department Development: Reflections from Australian Universities." Paper presented at the International Consortium for Educational Development conference, Austin, Tex., Apr. 1998.

Ho, A. "A Conceptual Change Staff Development Program: Effects as Perceived by Participants." *International Journal for Academic Development,* 1998, *3,* 24–38.

Jenkins, A. "Discipline-Based Educational Development." *International Journal for Academic Development,* 1996, *1,* 50–62.

Kember, D. "A Reconceptualization of the Research into University Academics' Conceptions of Teaching." *Learning and Instruction,* 1997, *7,* 255–275.

Laurillard, D. *Rethinking University Teaching.* London: Routledge, 1993.

McAlpine, L., and Harris, R. "Lessons Learned: Faculty Developer and Engineer Working as Faculty Development Colleagues." *International Journal of Academic Development,* 1999, *4,* 11–17.

Murray, H. "Does Evaluation of Teaching Lead to Improvement of Teaching?" *International Journal for Academic Development,* 1997, *2,* 8–23.

Ramsden, P. *Learning to Teach in Higher Education.* London: Routledge, 1992.

Saroyan, A., Amundsen, C., and Li, C. "Incorporating Theories of Teacher Growth and Adult Education in a Faculty Development Program." *To Improve the Academy,* 1997, *16,* 93–116.

Shulman, L. "Knowledge in Teaching: Foundations of the New Reform." *Harvard Educational Review,* 1987, *57,* 1–12.

Shulman, L. "Teaching as Community Property: Putting an End to Pedagogical Solitude." *Change,* 1993, 25 (6), 67.

Weimer, M., and Lenze, L. "Instructional Interventions: A Review of the Literature on Efforts to Improve Instruction." In K. A. Feldman and M. B. Paulsen (eds.), *Teaching and Learning in the College Classroom.* New York: Simon & Schuster, 1994.

CYNTHIA WESTON and LYNN MCALPINE are associate professors in the Department of Educational and Counselling Psychology at McGill University in Montreal and staff of McGill's Centre for University Teaching and Learning.

10

What are some of the key resources available to support the work of instructional consultants?

Resources on Instructional Consultation

Sergio Piccinin, Christopher Knapper

As the articles in this volume attest, instructional consultation can refer to a variety of activities carried out by individuals with different backgrounds and levels of preparation, from professional instructional developers to largely untrained peer consultants. Similarly the instructional consultation activities can vary from informal conversations with colleagues to more extensive consultations involving preliminary interviews followed by a variety of data collection activities, discussion, feedback, and follow-up sessions.

In this closing chapter we present a number of published resources useful to any professor, whether peer or professional instructional developer, interested in helping others to develop and enhance their teaching skills. The literature on instructional consultation has been growing by leaps and bounds in recent years, so of necessity we excluded (with a few exceptions) journal articles and locally published reports or manuals that are not in the public domain. Instead the emphasis is on major books, monographs, and some key periodicals, as well as associations or interest groups of special significance in this field. This is not an exhaustive list of resources. Rather, the intention is to refer to a selection of key documents. A number of the items we mention here have already been referenced in the earlier chapters. Our intention here is to highlight those we regard as the most important and useful to interested faculty, administrators, and educational developers, whether they are new to the field or experienced instructional consultants.

First, we describe a number of resources related to consultation *in general*. There follows a set of references more specifically related to *instructional* consultation and then a series of sources that deal with the *effects* of instructional consultation. Finally, we list a number of helpful monographs and other documents on instructional consultation and teaching improvement.

We are conscious of the fact that most of the references included here are American, mainly because instructional consulting has flourished in U.S. higher education, and there is a range of widely available publications on the topic. This issue of *NDTL* describes a number of interesting consultation approaches in other countries, but detailed published descriptions are generally unavailable. A case in point is the peer consultation approach developed at the University of Alberta, which has been described in local manuals not available for distribution to the wider public. We invite readers who know about resources that might be added to our list to write to the editors.

Resources on Consultation in General

Egan, G. *The Skilled Helper: A Problem-Management Approach to Helping.* (6th ed.) Pacific Grove, Calif.: Brooks/Cole, 1998.

There is extensive literature on the topic of helping. A reference that we particularly like is one of Gerard Egan's series on helping behavior. Accompanied by a workbook of exercises in helping skills, this is an excellent introduction to the activity of helping others in a variety of situations. The problem-management approach Egan employs is one that would appeal to professors interested in improving some aspects of their teaching.

Blake, R. R., and Mouton, J. S. *Consultation: A Handbook for Individual and Organization Development.* Reading, Mass.: Addison-Wesley, 1983.

Shein, E. H. *Process Consultation: Its Role in Organizational Development.* Reading, Mass.: Addison-Wesley, 1969.

The literature on consulting and the consulting process is also voluminous. Two frequently referenced books on consulting are E. H. Shein's *Process Consultation* and R. R. Blake and J. S. Mouton's *Consultation*. Both are useful, readable books. A significant contribution of Blake and Mouton is their managerial grid, which is useful for understanding the behavior of leaders as well as instructors.

Argyris, C., and Schön, D. *Theory in Practice: Increasing Professional Effectiveness.* San Francisco: Jossey-Bass, 1975.

Schön, D. *Educating the Reflective Practitioner: Toward a New Design for Teaching and Learning in the Professions.* San Francisco: Jossey-Bass, 1988.

The work of Chris Argyris and Donald Schön also deserves mention, notably their first publication, a classic, *Theory in Practice* and Schön's *Educating the Reflective Practitioner.* Although these books do not provide direction on how to do consultation, they have had a major impact on the preparation of professionals and the use of reflective practice to develop professional skills. Argyris and Schön are justly famous in the fields of business, management training, education, and counselor training. Their ideas on reflective practice have been widely influential and provide an invaluable theoretical underpinning for the process of consultation and for the consultant's ongoing professional development.

Gollessich, J. *The Handbook for Consultants, Trainers of Consultants, and Consumers of Consultation Services.* San Francisco: Jossey-Bass, 1982.
    Another volume worth exploring is this one by Judy Gollessich. This comprehensive volume outlines the different types of consultants and their basic roles and functions. Consultant roles are contrasted with those of other helping professionals such as supervisors and teachers. Although there is discussion of consulting with individuals, the major thrust of the volume is on professional consulting in organizations.

Block, P. *Flawless Consulting: A Guide to Getting Your Expertise Used.* Austin, Tex.: Learning Concepts, 1981.
    Written in a more practical vein is Peter Block's *Flawless Consulting.* This is clearly a how-to book. It is literal and practical, often suggesting specific things to say and do when dealing with individuals or groups.

Wergin, J. F. *Consulting in Higher Education: Principles for Institutions and Consultants.* Washington, D.C.: Association of American Colleges, 1989.
    Our final recommendation in this section is this small but useful volume on consulting in higher education. This guide is written for educational consultants as well as for college administrators interested in engaging their services. Although primarily concerned with institutional rather than individual teaching consultation issues, many of the points raised can be usefully transferred to the situation of instructional consultation. The chapter in which Wergin presents ten principles for consultants is particularly applicable.

Sourcebooks on Instructional Consultation

While most of the books in the field are written with the professional instructional consultant in mind, many of the strategies suggested can be employed by peer and professional consultants alike. We recommend the resources described below to anyone conducting instructional consultation.

Bergquist, W. H., and Phillips, S. R. *A Handbook for Faculty Development.* 2 vols. Washington, D.C.: Council for the Advancement of Small Colleges, 1975, 1977.
    We begin with the work of W. H. Bergquist and S. R. Phillips. These two volumes have become classics in the field. They provide a wealth of theory

as well as many practical suggestions that consultants can use to enhance the instructional and personal development of faculty.

Wadsworth, E. C. (ed.). *A Handbook for New Practitioners*. Stillwater, Okla.: New Forums Press/Professional and Organizational Development Network in Higher Education, 1988.

More recent resources are all published by New Forums Press, many of them referenced in earlier chapters. Among the best is *A Handbook for New Practitioners*, edited by E. Wadsworth, which continues to be a mainstay for new instructional consultants. An opening section provides an overview of the field of professional and organizational development; there are helpful sections on tools for the practitioner, a major section on strategies for working with individuals, and finally a section on working with groups.

Lewis, K. (ed.). *Face to Face: A Sourcebook of Individual Consultation Techniques for Faculty/Instructional Developers*. Stillwater, Okla.: New Forums Press, 1988.

Another very useful New Forums publication is *Face to Face,* edited by Karron Lewis. This book is aimed at novice and expert consultants alike. In three parts the book deals with general skills and philosophies of consultation, some specific methods of consultation for instructional improvement, and consultation in professional development. The middle and most lengthy section explores a variety of individual consulting methods that would be particularly helpful for instructional consultants.

Edington, S., and Hunt, C. *The Teaching Consultation Process Sourcebook*. Stillwater, Okla.: New Forums Press, 1996.

The Teaching Consultation Process Sourcebook was prepared for the University of Kentucky consultant program described in Kerwin's chapter in this issue. The program is organized around eighteen groups of behaviors that research has shown to be important to faculty and students. The sourcebook contains a chapter on each skill and includes definitions of each behavior, an overview of information available, current literature on the topic, and practical ways to help faculty improve their instruction in that area. The authors claim that this book focuses on behaviors that are most susceptible to change by the instructor, and it certainly provides many practical ideas and excellent references.

Brinko, K. T., and Menges, R. J. (eds.). *Practically Speaking: A Sourcebook for Instructional Consultants in Higher Education*. Stillwater, Okla.: New Forums Press, 1997.

Perhaps the most helpful major sourcebook, *Practically Speaking* is the result of editorial collaboration between Kathleen Brinko and Robert Menges. Their work includes thirty-seven chapters, all except one written expressly for the book. Written by a veritable who's who in instructional development, the chapters are grouped around five themes: skills and techniques of instructional consultation, programmatic approaches to instructional consultation, the context of consultation, evaluating consultation, and training instructional consultants. This volume should be on the shelf of every instructional consultant, and we concur with Menges's comment that the book offers a thoughtful blend of research-based principles and practical advice. Its only shortcoming is the absence of any discussion of the many ethical issues that arise in individual consultation.

Chism, N.V.N. *Peer Review of Teaching: A Sourcebook.* Bolton, Mass.: Anker, 1999.
     Finally, another very recent addition to the literature is Nancy Chism's *Peer Review of Teaching.* The first part consists of an overview of peer review, with chapters covering the rationale for peer review; setting up a peer review system; and the roles, goals, and focus of a peer review system. Part two of the book offers resources and guidelines on peer review of course materials, classroom observation, leadership in teaching, and teaching portfolios. A concluding chapter summarizes what Chism refers to as "habits of heart" required to make peer review successful whether undertaken to assist a colleague, to benefit the institution, or to aid one's own professional development. We are certain her sourcebook will be widely used.

Material on the Effectiveness of Instructional Consultation

The question of the effectiveness of instructional consultation is a critical one in these days of diminishing resources and increased calls for accountability. There is need for more research in this area, particularly to identify what factors in the consultation process are most influential in bringing about positive change and for whom.

Cohen, P. "Effectiveness of Student-Rating Feedback for Improving College Instruction: A Meta-Analysis of Findings." *Research in Higher Education,* 1980, *13,* 321–341.

Aleamoni, L., and Stevens, J. "The Effectiveness of Consultation in Support of Student Evaluation Feedback: A Ten-Year Follow-Up." Paper presented at the annual meeting of the Rocky Mountain Psychological Association, Albuquerque, N.M., Apr.–May 1983.
     The chapter by Piccinin in this issue provides a list of key references to studies of the effectiveness of instructional consultation. Of the various references listed there we would particularly recommend the following. Peter Cohen's "Effectiveness of Student-Rating Feedback for Improving College Instruction" is perhaps the most often cited paper on the effects of consultation. It highlights the impact on teaching improvement of

consultation in combination with student rating feedback. A paper by L. Aleamoni and J. Stevens, "The Effectiveness of Consultation in Support of Student Evaluation Feedback: A Ten-Year Follow-Up," is notable because it provides the longest follow-up of the effects of consultation.

Menges, R. J., and Brinko, K. T. "Effects of Student Evaluation Feedback: A Meta-Analysis of Higher Education Research." Paper presented at the 71st annual meeting of the American Educational Research Association, Washington, D.C., Apr. 1986.

This paper by R. J. Menges and K. T. Brinko is a further meta-analysis largely confirming the results described by Cohen.

L'Hommedieu, R., Menges, R. J., and Brinko, K. T. "Methodological Explanations for the Modest Effects of Feedback from Student Ratings." *Journal of Educational Psychology*, 1990, 82 (2), 232–241.

Our final key paper on this topic provides an incisive analysis of the problems and issues when researching the effects of consultation on teaching improvement (problems that Piccinin's study attempts to overcome).

Periodicals, Series, and Other Reference Sources on Instructional Consultation

The following periodicals are well-known outlets for the publication of articles relevant to instructional consultation: *College Teaching; International Journal for Academic Development; Journal of Educational Psychology; Journal of Higher Education; Journal of Staff, Program, and Organization Development; Journal on Excellence in College Teaching; Research in Higher Education; Review of Educational Research*; and *Training and Development Journal*. All have published papers on instructional consultation in the recent past. We do not give full details here, but you should be able to find many of them in your university library or teaching and learning center.

The Jossey-Bass New Directions for Teaching and Learning series is another valued resource for instructional consultants. This volume is a case in point. Another is *Effective Practices for Improving Teaching*, edited by M. Theall and J. Franklin (no. 48, Winter 1991).

The series sponsored by the Professional and Organizational Development Network in Higher Education (POD), *To Improve the Academy*, has been published annually since 1982 and is also a valuable resource. Each issue contains many articles of interest to instructional consultants; copies are available from New Forums Press, Stillwater, Oklahoma.

Another useful series for instructional consultants is the ASHE-ERIC Higher Education Reports, published by George Washington University. A recent example is *Taking Teaching Seriously: Meeting the Challenge of Instructional Improvement*, by M. B. Paulsen and K. Feldman (ASHE-ERIC Higher Education Report No. 2. Washington, D.C.: George Washington University, Graduate School of Education and Human Development, 1995). This volume examines the features of a university culture that support teaching and also reviews theory and research relative to helping faculty improve teaching quality. It is an excellent resource for instructional consultants.

Finally, another recent publication is that of Alan Wright and Associates, *Teaching Improvement Practices: Successful Strategies for Higher Education* (Bolton, Mass.: Anker, 1995). This book examines recent initiatives to enhance teaching, drawing on experiences in North America, the United Kingdom, and Australia. It provides thoughtful reflection and professional insight on educational development activities and is a useful reference for instructional consultants.

Professional Organizations Concerned with Instructional Consultation

There are a number of associations and organizations concerned with university teaching and development that offer resources and information of use to instructional consultants. These are described more fully in the penultimate chapter of Brinko and Menges's *Practically Speaking,* mentioned earlier in this chapter.

At least two North American associations, POD in the United States and the Society for Teaching and Learning in Higher Education (STLHE) in Canada sponsor electronic discussion forums (listservs). Anyone seeking an answer to an instructional or consulting question can post a message by electronic mail and receive helpful suggestions. The ongoing discussions of issues on these listservs are useful to college teachers as well as to peer or professional instructional consultants. Still another discussion list is the Deliberations listserv sponsored by the Staff Educational Development Association (SEDA) in the United Kingdom.

In addition to interesting exchanges on myriad teaching topics, these lists include useful discussions on principles and practices of effective instructional consultation. Recent debates on such topics as starting and ending courses, managing incivility in the classroom, and helping an apparently very bad teacher allow participants to focus on sound teaching principles and practice as well as on the process of instructional consulting.

There is no fee for subscribing to the listservs, and you do not have to be a member of the sponsoring society to join the discussion forum. To subscribe, send an e-mail message as outlined here to the relevant listserv address. In each case leave the subject line of your message blank.

- Address for POD: pod-request@iastate.edu
Message: Subscribe pod your email address

- Address for STLHE: listserv@listserv.unb.ca
Message: Subscribe STLHE-L your first name, your second name.

- Address for Deliberations: mailbox@mailbox.ac.uk
Message: Join deliberations-forum, first name, last name

SERGIO PICCININ is professor of psychology and director of the Centre for University Teaching Development at the University of Ottawa, Canada.

CHRISTOPHER KNAPPER is professor of psychology and director of the Centre for University Teaching at Queen's University, Kingston, Canada.

INDEX

Back Issue/Subscription Order Form

Copy or detach and send to:
Jossey-Bass Inc., Publishers, 350 Sansome Street, San Francisco CA 94104-1342

Call or fax toll free!
Phone 888-378-2537 6AM-5PM PST; Fax 800-605-2665

Back issues: Please send me the following issues at $23 each
(Important: please include series initials and issue number, such as TL90)

1. TL _____

_____

_____

$ _____ Total for single issues

$ _____ Shipping charges (for single issues **only;** subscriptions are exempt from shipping charges): Up to $30, add $5^{50} • $30^{01}–$50, add $6^{50} $50^{01}–$75, add $7^{50} • $75^{01}–$100, add $9 • $100^{01}–$150, add $10 Over $150, call for shipping charge

Subscriptions   Please ❏ start   ❏ renew my subscription to *New Directions for Teaching and Learning* for the year 19___ at the following rate:

❏ Individual $58   ❏ Institutional $104
NOTE: Subscriptions are quarterly, and are for the calendar year only. Subscriptions begin with the spring issue of the year indicated above. For shipping outside the U.S., please add $25.

$ _____ Total single issues and subscriptions (CA, IN, NJ, NY and DC residents, add sales tax for single issues. NY and DC residents must include shipping charges when calculating sales tax. NY and Canadian residents only, add sales tax for subscriptions)

❏ Payment enclosed (U.S. check or money order only)

❏ VISA, MC, AmEx, Discover Card #_____ Exp. date_____

Signature _____ Day phone _____

❏ Bill me (U.S. institutional orders only. Purchase order required)

Purchase order #_____

Name _____

Address _____

_____

_____

Phone_____ E-mail _____

For more information about Jossey-Bass Publishers, visit our Web site at:
www.josseybass.com   **PRIORITY CODE = ND1**